ALSO BY NATALIE GOLDBERG

Writing Down the Bones
Wild Mind
Long Quiet Highway
Banana Rose
Living Color

THUNDER AND LIGHTNING

Cracking Open the Writer's Craft

NATALIE GOLDBERG

BANTAM BOOKS
New York Toronto London Sydney Auckland

This edition contains the complete text
of the original hardcover edition.
NOT ONE WORD HAS BEEN OMITTED.

THUNDER AND LIGHTNING

PUBLISHING HISTORY
Bantam hardcover edition published August 2000
Bantam trade paperback edition / November 2001

Book design by Casey Hampton

Library of Congress Catalog Card Number: 00-029746

ISBN 0-553-37496-6

Published simultaneously in the United States and Canada

Bantam Books are published by Bantam Books, a division of Random House, Inc. Its trademark, consisting of the words "Bantam Books" and the portrayal of a rooster, is Registered
in U.S. Patent and Trademark Office and in other countries. Marca Registrada. Bantam
Books, 1540 Broadway, New York, New York 10036.

PRINTED IN THE UNITED STATES OF AMERICA

BVG   10   9   8   7   6   5   4   3   2   1

THIS BOOK IS DEDICATED TO

Allen Ginsberg (1926–1997)
who started me on the path of writing and the mind

and

Toni Burbank
who helped me to refine that path

ACKNOWLEDGMENTS

The author would like to acknowledge Susan Guillaume, Frances Kean, Eddie Lewis and John Thorndike, who patiently and faithfully read through an earlier draft of this manuscript; Jean Leyshon, dharma friend and all-around assistant, who typed this manuscript; Dennis Leri, whose apartment I stayed in while I wrote the initial draft; Wendy Johnson, fellow writer to whom I read aloud chapters of this book at D'Angelo's in Mill Valley, California; Barry Williams, dream guide in Taos Canyon; Alfred Padilla, old Farmingdale classmate who reminded me of the name of our ninth-grade biology teacher; Maria Fortin and the rest of the staff at the Mabel Dodge Luhan House; Sam & Eddie's Open Books in Yellow Springs, Ohio, who researched copyrights for me; Antioch College, where I did a writer's residency and a final polish on this manuscript; Nita Sweeney, loyal and dedicated student; Sean Murphy, friend and workshop assistant; Jim Plumeri, with whom I've had the pleasure to work on all my book covers; and Jisho Warner, for meticulous editorial help in preparing the final manuscript.

To Dosho Mike Port, a huge thank-you, and to Michele Huff, my beloved partner and deep, supportive friend, much appreciation.

To the memory of my sweet, lovable Uncle Manny Edman (1907–1999).

To the memory of my father, Benjamin Goldberg (1916–1999)—there are no words for the depth of my love.

CONTENTS

WARNING!

I HAVE NOT SEEN WRITING lead to happiness in my friends' lives. I'm sorry to say this, I, who just fifteen years ago published a book telling everyone to grab their notebooks and write their asses off. No high like it, I said. I meant it—and it was true. Now I'm past fifty, and I have given everything to writing, the way a Zen master watches her breath and burns through distraction. Was I a fool to do this? Did I choose the wrong path?

I once told my great teacher Katagiri Roshi, "If I put the effort into zazen that I put into writing, I'd be sitting where you are."

"Yes, yes," he beamed.

But I didn't. Whatever small insight I eked out, whatever breakdown of illusion I realized or moment I stepped outside ego's poisons, I dedicated wholeheartedly to illuminating the writing path.

Eight years after my first book came out—I'd written three others in that time—I was sitting a Zen practice period in California. For eight weeks we woke up at five AM, meditated for several hours each day, worked in the fields, studied, chanted, listened to lectures. Every week we had an individual meeting with the abbot,

1

who was Norm Fischer, a friend of mine and also a serious poet. During the third week, when it was my turn to go in and speak with him, I said, "Norm, when I sit a lot, as I'm doing now, what comes up, way down at the bottom, is that my heart is still broken from bringing out *Writing Down the Bones*. I've done therapy, I've learned good professional boundaries——"

"But you handle your success, you've helped so many——"

I cut him off. "I want you to hear me. Below all that, when I'm in this zendo day after day all I feel is an aching. I was so innocent—I didn't know what it meant to put my heart in the marketplace."

A long silence. I knew this time he'd heard me.

"You know," he said, "what I've seen—and this comes from my own close observations—is art leads to suffering. I have a lot of poet friends. The ones who've made it seem miserable. And the ones who haven't—when I go to visit them they whip out a newly published anthology and point out a poem: 'See, this isn't as good as mine and he's getting published.' Luckily, you have a foot in another world, Zen, so you won't get swallowed up."

I wasn't so sure. I had been certain art would save me. I knew all my writing friends felt the same way. After all, what could be better? I thought back to the first poem I'd ever written, about an Ebinger's blackout cake. In the shine of the icing, I saw God. I'd never felt so complete as I did that afternoon writing on my bed in Ann Arbor, Michigan. I poured my soul out on the page and it shimmered back at me.

And now this? Art leads to suffering? But it was true. I'd seen it again and again. Why hadn't any of us realized it? Why hadn't we put on the brakes? All my friends had tasted the sweetness of writing. Aflame with longing to make our mark, we didn't know what lay ahead: dislocation, isolation.

Months later back in Taos I called my friend Eddie, who was diligently working on his second novel. "Yeah," he sighed. "I don't know any writer who's happy. But what else is there to do?"

"I know what you mean," I said. "If there's any clear steering in this life for me, it will be through writing. But knowing what we know, how can I encourage people any more? I wanted my work to help people, give them clarity, not make them sad and desolate."

We laughed and then I told him, "I was reduced to going to *Space Jam* with Michael Jordan and Bugs Bunny last Sunday for some inspiration. I'm trying to start a new book."

"Well, you seem to be following the right leads," he chortled.

I told him how I loved Sir Altitude and that I thought maybe the greatest athlete in the world could make me believe in writing again. "You know, when I first saw him play I thought that Jordan had everything to do with Zen—one-pointed, alert, present, alive. Years later when I was on a book tour in Chicago I went to the hotel bar after my reading. Everyone was crowded around the TV. Master Air had just returned to basketball. It was his second game and he broke his scoring record. The next day they had a poll: should Michael Jordan be declared King of the World? Reading the newspaper in the elevator, I blurted out, 'Absolutely!' "

"Well, did *Space Jam* inspire you?" Eddie came back to the point.

"Not really," I said.

That night after talking to Eddie I couldn't sleep. At three AM I got out of bed and went into the living room to sit zazen. I said to myself, OK, Nat, every cell in your body gets it now—sooner or later you're going to die. You've made a lot of foolish mistakes, maybe writing was a dumb dream, but so what. Being a doctor, a rock star, a mother would have led to the same thing.

Then I paused and asked myself, Nat, are you depressed?

I sat with moonlight streaming through my big windows and

filling the mesa with a silver light. I saw a jackrabbit dash through the sage.

No, I thought, I'm not depressed. I hesitated: I'm the most peaceful I've ever been. It was true. I felt a vast acceptance of everything.

A small voice then asked, Well, now do you think you can write this book?

The title *Thunder and Lightning* had come to me two years earlier as I stood in awe at the foot of Arenal, an active volcano in Costa Rica. It was a perfectly clear day; then across the sky flew dark clouds, flashes of light, tremendous sound as though rock cliffs had exploded, followed by a downpour that abruptly turned the jungle slate-gray. I stood under my black umbrella near the protection of a cinder-block wall and watched. Wind howled through trees, and the rain, twice changing directions, first pelted the sides and then the front of my legs. Suddenly everything became soft, quiet, dripping, drenched, thick and muggy—and cracks of blue appeared in the sky overhead.

I thought, some divine structure has just whipped through here. That which manifests from nothing, changes everything and then is gone.

Wasn't that how I had created book after book in the past ten years? Where did they come from, how did I figure out how to build them? They presented themselves, I was absorbed; they were finished and I was left empty-handed.

My eye caught another fast movement outside the living room windows. Was it a coyote?—no, my neighbor's white dog was prowling near the big piñon. Last week he'd dug up my compost heap. I took a deep breath. I remembered a Sunday a month earlier when my friend Frances had driven up from Santa Fe to see me. Sundays in Taos can be the worst days, especially in late fall with no tourists on the streets. The place looks deserted, a ghost town with nothing moving. I can settle into a deep desolation on those days. When I met Frances behind the Café Tazza I could tell she felt as bad as I did.

"Let's climb Divisadero, straight up. No stopping." I thought breathing heavily up a steep incline would help.

After an hour and a half, heaving at the top, I turned to her. "Any better?"

She shook her head.

"Me neither." As we climbed down, I suggested we go to my house and sit zazen. The blues were thick in the car as we drove across the mesa.

I rang the bell to start the meditation. We sat till the incense burned down, a full hour.

As I unfolded my legs, I looked at her. I already knew the answer, but I asked, "How do you feel now?"

"Bad."

"Me, too." Neither hiking nor meditating had shifted the energy of our Sunday doldrums. I finally gave in and suggested the one thing I didn't want to suggest—I'd been struggling with writing all that past week. "OK, let's try writing practice."

We wrote for half an hour, read to each other, wrote another half hour, read aloud.

By the end we were both beaming. Writing practice had done it again—digested our sorrow, dissolved and integrated our inner rigidity, and let us move on. I don't even remember what we wrote about. It didn't matter. The effort of forming words, physically connecting hand with mind and heart, and then having the freedom to read aloud transformed us.

Yes, writing practice is good. It can help people, but I'm not so sure about taking it further.

I ask myself, OK, Nat, what's been good about writing books these last ten years?

I begin to enumerate—I'm not naive about publishing, I make a living—and suddenly stop. Wait a minute! Now I really remember something. In writing practice I am still following a trail of desire, indulging my own wandering mind. But when I write a book I surrender not to the liberal travels of my restless thoughts but to the design of the work itself. I harness the energy of wild mind to serve the ancient demands of structure—demands that are larger than myself and deeper in the matrix of the human mind. Writing a book is my one chance to experience freedom, to cut loose by succumbing to the discipline of form. It is an opportunity to touch something holy—like that storm in Costa Rica—independent of my human ego.

To rid myself of myself and my own wild cry for attention, I realize, is no less demanding than what it would have been like for me to sit in a cold zendo day after day.

I never escaped being a monk! The morning gruel, the frost on the bell, bare feet on frigid floors, all have been mine. Except that my meditation position has been a bent body hovering over a notebook with only my right hand moving across a blank page for hours at a time.

I know no one wants to hear me say how hard writing is—quit while you can. In the Japanese monasteries they warn you not to come in. In fact, you have to prove your sincerity and mettle by sitting outside the gates day after day before you can be admitted.

Shunryu Suzuki Roshi once sent an energetic but uppity San Francisco Zen Center student to a monastery outside Kyoto. They had him sit for five days outside the wall, and then he was called in for an interview. The teacher handed him a paper and pencil: "Write your name."

He did what he was told and handed it back. The teacher looked at the paper. "Please continue to sit."

After five more days, he was called in again. "Write your name."

He wrote his name and once more was sent outside.

The eleventh day, the twelfth day—the same. On the thirteenth day, the Zen teacher again asked the young American to write his name.

He picked up the pencil, put it to paper, paused, looked up, looked back down, looked up at the teacher. "I can't. I don't know how."

"Good. You're ready to enter."

So here I am—I hope not too late. Do not say you were not warned: to continue this crazy thing called writing might lead to steep precipices, dangerous canyons, craggy cliffs. I make no promises.

A student in a workshop walked up to me swinging his briefcase. "Hi, I'm an engineer. I make forty-six thousand dollars a year. How long do you think it will take me to earn that much with writing?"

"Keep your job," I told him. Now I think if that student comes by again, I'll screech in bloodcurdling syllables, "No advances! No assurances! No credentials! No merit!"

Know that you will eventually have to leave everything behind; the writing will demand it of you. Bareboned, you are on the path with no markers, only the skulls of those who never made it back. But I have made the journey, and I have made it back—over and over again. I will act as your guide.

Now that you have been warned, let me also say this: if you want to know what you're made of, if you want to stand on death's dark face and leave behind the weary yellow coat of yourself, then just now—I hear it—the heavy wooden doors of the cloister of no return are creaking open. Please enter.

Part One

STRUCTURE

MEETING THE MIND

BACK IN NINTH-GRADE BIOLOGY CLASS when Mr. Albert Tint announced that we would study the involuntary organs—the heart and lungs—he forgot to mention the mind. My guess is he didn't know about it, but in truth it's as though the brain were an automatic thought-producing machine—I don't like this dress. I'm hungry. I miss New York. How did I get so old? I wonder where I put my keys? Did I mail that letter? I need to cut my nails. Next time I'm going to buy a car with automatic transmission. I hope I didn't bounce my last check. Maybe I should try acupuncture—just like the popcorn machine in the movie theatre lobby that explodes kernel after kernel.

What's remarkable is that before I sat meditation and tried to focus on my breath when I was twenty-six years old, I didn't know this about my mind: that I couldn't stop it from thinking. I was full of arrogance in my twenties. I thought there was nothing I couldn't do. And then I discovered I wasn't in control.

The first morning of my first retreat I woke early—it was still dark—dressed quickly and went to the meditation kiva, a small mud room, on the side of Lama Mountain, seventeen miles north of Taos, New Mexico. The bell rang—we were to sit still and focus our attention on the breath. What breath? I couldn't find it. Instead I was plunged into a constant yammering. Rushes of thought ran through me. Endless commentary, opinions, ideas, stories. The bell rang a half hour later to signal the end of the period. Wow! I opened my eyes. Who was that wild animal inside me?

It was my own human mind. I needed to understand it. Why? It's the writer's landscape. Imagine that a painter has that wild animal to capture on canvas: arresting its fangs, the raging color of its eyes, the blue of its hump, the flash of its hoofs, the rugged shadow that it casts. We writers have that beast inside us: how we feel, think, hope, dream, perceive. Where do words come from, sentences, ideas? They manifest from our minds. Yikes! Suddenly we're blasted into a vast jungle, with no maps, no guidelines, no clues. How do we manifest a landscape so full of robust life? What do we say? When there's so much—it's boundless—we usually close down, disconnect, shut up.

That's how I was anyway: confused. I knew my teachers in public school were trying to teach me something—mainly, they were good, earnest people. But I couldn't figure out, not even a hint, how a writer wrote. I managed to squeeze out dry little compositions; nothing burst into flame. Carson McCullers, Steinbeck, Joyce—the writers we studied were a million miles away from me. How did they do it? They might as well have been nuclear scientists. Yet they possessed the same things I did: pen, paper, English language, mind.

My teachers couldn't teach me because they hadn't connected with writing's essential ingredient: the mind and how it functions. Instead, they taught me how to organize what was outside and around the pulsing lifeblood. I learned to make an outline, but that skeletal plan was built exterior to the heat of creation. Why was this? Western intelligence, preoccupied with thinking, avoided examining the mechanism of thought. Only saints or the insane traveled that interior territory. And what was the result? They cut off their ears, shot themselves, or were burned at the stake. Better not go there. We looked suspiciously on the inner world. It wasn't productive: it could lead only to suffering or turning nutty as a fruitcake. We in the West were better at developing athletes. We knew about bodies.

But then suddenly in the sixties large numbers of young Americans ingested psychedelics, which blasted us inward. Wanting to understand what we experienced with these "mind altering" drugs, we turned to Eastern religions to find answers.

What the East gave the West was a safe, structured way to explore the mind. Those of us who sought meditation were taught a fundamental, disciplined posture. The directions were specific: cross legs, sit at the edge of a hard round cushion, hands on knees or held just below the navel, chest open, crown of the head a little higher than the forehead, eyes cast down and unfocused. When the bell rings, do not move. Go! And where did we go? Noplace, at least externally. The instruction was to pay attention to our breath, but as soon as we tried we found instead hurricanes of thoughts and emotions—rebellion, desire, restlessness, agitation.

It was all I could do to sit still. Suddenly I wanted to sob at the memory of my grandmother and the feel of her thin skin; I recalled why my tenth-grade boyfriend had dropped me ten years earlier, and how it felt when the novocaine on my first root canal ran out while Dr. Glassman was still drilling. No wonder our schoolteachers stayed away from the meat of writing. To have us contact our raw minds in class would have incited immediate chaos: hordes of teenagers bolting from their neat rows of wooden desks and dashing for the water fountains as though the roots of their hair were on fire.

But with meditation we found a steady tool to enter this wild space and explore it. The sitting bell rang again, marking the end of the period. We uncurled our legs and looked around. The earth was still patiently beneath us, and we had had a small opening—say, thirty minutes—to taste our minds. Zen was smart: it did not just lower us into the hot water and leave us there to boil. We were dipped in and out. We went under and then came back up to sip green tea and munch cookies. In this way we slowly cooked and digested ourselves.

There was another reason some of us were drawn to Zen meditation. It told us what to do: wear black in the zendo, bow to your cushion, don't make any noise, be on your seat five minutes before the beginning of a sitting session. After an initial rebellious tantrum where I walked out of the instruction class, I loved it. I longed for order. My guess is others in my generation craved that, too. I had had a laissez-faire upbringing. As a child I lounged around the kitchen eating boxes of Oreo cookies. My mother simply walked by, patted me on the head, and commented, "That's nice, dear." I missed at least one day of school a week. "I just don't feel like going," I'd tell my mother, looking up from under the bedsheets. She nodded, endlessly understanding, turned around in her housecoat and left the room. "Natli doesn't learn that much there anyway," I could hear her thinking. I sat in front of the TV all weekend in my pajamas. No rules, no requirements. On my own I decided it might be a good idea to brush my teeth and wash my face once a day.

When my friends hear this they feel envy: "Why, it's ideal for raising a writer." Not true. Life was staggering. I needed organization. And the sixties didn't help. Those years only made me more confused instead of free. In Zen there were precepts: Don't lie. Don't steal. Don't create suffering through sexuality. That one I read over and over. I wasn't sure what it meant, but at least there was a scent of guidance, an intimation of direction.

So when I tried to figure out how to write—living in a small adobe in New Mexico, the clear Western skies out my window, the land spotted by sage, bare yellow dirt everywhere and three horses in a corral—I looked to the Eastern world for hints. I copied the structure of meditation. Sitting had a time limit—OK, writing would, too. At the beginning I wrote for rounds of ten minutes, eventually increasing them to twenty and thirty. I kept my hand consistently moving—as in meditation we couldn't move—for the full time. I told myself if the atom bomb dropped eight minutes after I began, I'd go out writing. (In recent years I have softened: I concede to my writing students, "Well, if you're writing with your best friend when the bomb drops, you might pause a moment to say good-bye. But then get going again—you don't have much time.")

Writing became a practice. I wrote under all circumstances, and once I started, I continued until the time was up. Especially in the early days, like Zen students who sit together, I wrote with others, not alone. I let Zen inform my writing practice because I needed writing to be rooted—not Natalie's creative idea. I wanted writing practice to be backed by two thousand years of watching the mind. Enough of my free-wheeling childhood. I was serious.

Years later at the Minnesota Zen Meditation Center where I studied with Dainin Katagiri Roshi, we chanted the lineage of teachers all the way back to Buddha. I learned that one Zen master lost his mother at nine; one was the son of a whore. My own teacher was the youngest of six children; they lived over a small noodle shop owned by his father. Nobody in the lineage began as someone special. I saw that the only way to elbow my way into the lineage of writers was by sincere effort. The fact that my father owned a bar, that my grandmother had plucked chickens in a poultry market, did not deter me. I understood that it was no more helpful to have a parent who was a well-known writer than to be the child of an army general. Actually I might be luckier with the general—then I wouldn't be working in my famous parent's shadow, my path darkened by my mother's successful novels. But no matter what, it was up to me.

I never gained control of my mind—how do you dominate an ocean?—but I began to form a real relationship with it. Through writing and meditation I identified monkey mind, that constant critic, commentator, editor, general slug and pain-in-the-ass, the voice that says, "I can't do this, I'm bored, I hate myself, I'm no good, I can't sit still, who do I think I am?" I saw that most of my life had been spent following that voice as though it were God, telling me the real meaning of life—"Natalie, you can't write shit"—when, in fact, it was a mechanical contraption that all human minds contain. Yes, even people with terrific, supportive parents are inhabited by this blabbing, resistant mouthpiece. But as I wrote longer, went deeper, I realized its true purpose: monkey mind is the guardian at the gate. We have to prove our mettle, our determination, stand up to its nagging, shrewish cry, before it surrenders the hidden jewels. And what are those jewels? Our own human core and heart, of course.

I've seen it over and over. The nearer I get to expressing my essence, the louder, more zealous that belittling voice becomes. It has been helpful to understand it not as a diminishing parent but as something universal, impersonal, a kind of spiritual test. Then I don't have to wither or sneak away from censoring dad, carping mom, or severe schoolteacher with sunken chest when I hear that onerous yell. Instead, it is my signal to persevere and plow through. Charge! I scream with pen unlanced.

But this intimacy with my mind did not come quickly and I never gained the upper hand. Instead I've learned to maneuver in the territory. It is something like when I first got my driver's license at eighteen. My father's big blue Buick convertible felt massive; it was like propelling Jell-O through the streets. If I smelled sulfur from a factory, or autumn leaves burning by the curb, I panicked and stomped on the brake, certain the car was on fire and about to blow up. Other than putting the key in the ignition, steering around corners, and turning on the lights and radio, I had no idea what to do with this enormous moving animal. Later, with the sprouting of feminism, I learned to change a tire, the oil, a filter. These things— plus I had more driving experience—gave me a closer relationship with this entity called an automobile.

In the same way in my late twenties as I continued to fill spiral notebooks in cafés all over Taos and to sit zazen in friends' early-morning gardens and in my thick-walled adobe, I developed a connection with my mind. But like a juniper's unhurried growth in the dry Southwest, the relationship matured slowly through the turning of many seasons.

HALLUCINATING EMERALDS

IN THE LATE SPRING OF 1978, as the green leaves finally broke through the heavy Midwest winter, I moved to Minneapolis to marry. I felt a new force in and around me. I walked the well-organized streets and city blocks and a desire woke: I wanted to record the writing odyssey I had been on and share with the world what I understood of practice and the mind. I was entrusting myself to marriage, why not commit my inner journey to the page? I would write a book!

I woke early and kissed my new husband good-bye. He was off to work. The morning sun splashed in the bedroom. I looked out the window: the street in front of our duplex was crowded with cars. Everyone had a job to go to—and suddenly I did, too! I rushed down to the Cedar-Riverside area of town and purchased a ream of white paper and a batch of fast-writing pens. Then I returned home and sat down behind a small wooden desk in front of a window in our living room to begin.

I wrote "when" in the upper left-hand corner of my page. Naa, I said to myself, you can't start a book with that. I sighed and crossed "when" out. I stared out the window. Deep maples lined the street. A short woman walked by with a dachshund on a leash. He barked and in a flash the word "while" came to me. I grabbed my pen and jotted it down. I paused, nothing else came. I heaved a deep breath and struck "while" out.

C'mon, Nat, I coached myself, start with the most proletarian word you can think of. I wrote "the" below the two other scratched-out words. Ahh, now I have something, I thought.

Then I looked out the window again. I hallucinated emeralds in the trees. I stared down the marigolds in my neighbor's yard and I cleaned my index fingernail with the cap of my pen. My eyes watered. The shadows shifted in the room. I was thirty years old, bored out of my skull. Two hours passed. A column of eight crossed-out words decorated a single page of paper. A day of writing was finished. I drifted over to the kitchen and made a shrimp-in-wine-sauce quiche for my new husband. This I liked. I had purpose; I felt alive again.

Each day I repeated the same ritual: I made it through several grueling hours of nothing happening, trying to write a book. It was as painful as the jobs I'd had as a kid. My first one, at sixteen, was selling sunglasses in freezing gray December at Abraham & Straus on Long Island. Everyone was crowded across the aisle at the wool socks and scarves. Waiting through endless hours, I tasted my first deep boredom. And now at the beginning of my fourth decade on earth I was experiencing the same unbearable ennui. After several weeks of this I wasn't drifting, I was dashing for the kitchen.

For years I'd bravely leaned in my sleeping bag against ponderosas in the New Mexico wilderness, propped myself at friends' kitchen tables, at counters in cheap restaurants and cafés, in the backseats of cars, pen in hand over my notebook, exploring the inner organic workings of my mind. I'd given myself permission to write the worst shit in America and the freedom not to worry about grammar, punctuation or spelling. Then, suddenly faced with the task of writing a book, I balked. I denied any true understanding I had about the writing process. Instead I reached way back through the years to grab the hem of my grammar-school teacher's skirt.

Mrs. Post was short and stout, the Napoleon of our grade school. What had she demanded of us? I frantically tried to remember. Before you start to write, make an outline: topics, subtopics, Roman numerals. Yes, yes, I could do that! and right there in my living room I made a sweeping capital I. Ah, those Romans, they would help me, I thought: Leonardo da Vinci, Michelangelo—even the pope! Then suddenly I felt crushed. That Roman number was too familiar—Mrs. Post's triumphant year slowly materialized before my eyes. There was eleven-year-old Natalie frozen at her desk unwilling to attempt any written expression whatsoever. All those rules had ruined her, and here I was so long after, trying to rely on the false security of my meanest schoolteacher in an effort to organize myself.

I even remembered young Natalie's answer to an early fall assignment: what did you do on your summer vacation? In a scrawny small script on blue lined paper I wrote: "I had a lot of fun. It was interesting. I liked it. It was nice." I cringed as I heard those words again in my home in Minneapolis.

If only I'd known then that I could write the real answer to that question: last summer my mother dyed her hair red. I think she was kissing the electrician. My father wore his underwear to dinner and drank beer, and my sister and I played checkers almost every afternoon in the garage. The days were hot. The evenings were no better and mosquitoes crawled through the screens and buzzed all night in the bedroom I shared with old Aunt Doris who snored and talked in her sleep.

But instead, so long after those deathly childhood compositions, I was transported in the first year of my marriage back to those barren school words—"nice," "interesting," "fun"—to try to explain the unbridled joy of writing I had experienced in the hills of Taos.

No wonder I quit. Pretty soon I had a small catering business issuing out of our modest flat. I'd do anything not to face that "book," the gray asphalt staring back at me through the front window, the cars zooming into the Conoco station across the way, and to my right out the other window Mr. Steak's blinking sign.

I quit because in truth I had no sense of how to begin a book or how to end one—when do you stop? I panicked. This writing could go on forever. And the middle of the book—that was even worse than the beginning or the end. How could I transport what was inside me to a form outside me? I was stumped.

I did not think of the book again for six years. Then one gray afternoon in March, I was sitting with my best writing buddy Kate Green in the Croissant Express in the Uptown area of Minneapolis, bemoaning my fate. By then I'd been writing poetry for almost thirteen years. I'd won a fellowship for a year and now it had run out. My first poetry book had been published, but I had a second manuscript of poetry no one wanted. I was tired of living at the periphery of society. I wanted people to read my words.

"Hey, Nat," she brightened. "Why don't you write that book you were planning to do when I first met you? You know, the one on writing practice."

I sat up in my chair—suddenly it seemed like such an original idea! I snapped off a cookie chunk and replied, "Yes!" just like that. No hesitation.

Kate finished her coffee and we hugged good-bye. I'm not sure my old friend was aware of what she had unleashed in me just then. I watched her as she walked out the door. Even through her heavy blue jacket I could see her strong, good back.

Evening swarmed across the immense Midwest sky as I drove through the green lights of Hennepin Avenue. I turned the corner at Thirty-first Street and before me flashed *Zen Mind, Beginner's Mind* by Shunryu Suzuki. That's it! I thought. That's how I'll write my book.

Suzuki Roshi's book was a series of short lectures. A reader could open to any one and get a taste of this Zen master's mind. I'd make my own chapters short; they wouldn't have to be read chronologically. After all, you couldn't learn about the mind consecutively, and neither could writing be taught linearly. The structure of the book would match the way my mind moved. A person reading the book would experience how writing practice unfolded when I was actually doing it.

Six years earlier when I'd first attempted to write the book, I hadn't even known it was structure I was looking for. But structure was the secret ingredient. Once I had a strong framework I could pour my wild mind into it, secure that something held it up. Upon this skeleton I could build a book. I suppose Mrs. Post was trying to give me a structure when she taught outlining, but that was an artificial support, something imposed from outside that couldn't contain the natural life of my mind.

Now I approached the book exactly the way I approached writing practice. Every time I thought of a topic or idea, any flash at all, even if it seemed to have no connection to writing—the apples in fall at Nora Zimmerman's orchard in Talpa or the story I'd heard about the man who ate a car in India—I jotted it down at the back of my notebook. Then when I sat down to write, I'd pick at random three or four topics from the back, list them at the top of a fresh piece of paper and say, "Go, write for two hours." The only rules: I'd somehow have to include all the topics listed at the top of the page, and the chapter had to disclose something about writing.

Often I began writing chapters with the actual present moment—where I was sitting, what was on the table, what I was wearing, how I felt, how the weather was outside. This helped to ground me. From there I took off into my wild mind, which was huge and included everything, so I had no trouble bringing together blue lipstick, a cheesecake, a chair and a Plymouth with a lesson on commitment in writing. The seemingly disconnected topics helped to energize the piece. They jolted my mind to display how it really skipped around—all the while staying connected and alive.

Now I felt excited when I sat down to write. Each chapter was an act of discovery rather than an act of manipulation. I was creating and developing the book organically in the same way I had taught myself to write. Now it was connected to the enormous vibrancy of wild mind. Unlike six years earlier, I wasn't trying to suppress my real mind to become someone else's idea of a writer.

When the thought of using Suzuki's structure sprang into my mind, it was organic to what I was trying to express and it was also organic to my life—I wasn't "ripping off" Suzuki. I'd read his book many times during the ten years since I'd begun to meditate. I'd never met him, but through reading him, I'd met his mind. For the past six years I had also been studying Zen intensively with Katagiri Roshi, who had taught with Suzuki in San Francisco before coming to Minneapolis. So the lineage, blood and action of Suzuki's book were integrated in my body. And then there were all those years I'd spent writing poetry. Wasn't a book of poetry similar to *Zen Mind, Beginner's Mind?* A poetry book can be opened to any poem to get a concentrated taste of the poet's mind. So Suzuki's structure was subliminally familiar to me.

An organic structure is aligned with who we are and what we have to say. It is not disconnected from ourself. If a form isn't organic, I think a great struggle ensues—the writer tries to stuff her being into a costume that doesn't fit. I knew that struggle well. I experienced it morning after morning during my first months in Minnesota. It is not an unusual battle. We often go against ourselves, out of ignorance or because of how we've been taught by society. So this is important for us to remember (I want to emblazon it on a tee-shirt, paint it across my bedroom ceiling): structure must be organic!

Meditation and writing practice point inward and offer a built-in form for meeting our true self. Then we're on our own. Each person has to find her way to meet the world and to carry that true self, what's inside, out into the flow of life and into her readers' minds.

We should keep our hand moving on the page and be patient to allow structure to meet us halfway. It's not our little will that will discover organic structure, but we also cannot sit idle. I know it sounds as though Suzuki's book descended from the heavens and hit me on the head that night in Uptown Minneapolis, but more likely, all those years something in me was seeking a way to write that book—I just wasn't ready. But I did continue to do writing practice, create poems and sit zazen. The moment I was ripe, I woke up and received the answer, plunged ahead and wrote the book. Now, looking back, I think that even those hours of boredom in my living room were not wasted.

OLD FRIEND FROM FAR AWAY

"WRITE WHAT YOU KNOW," beginning writers are repeatedly told. They think, OK, I'll tell about my life, I know that. They begin: "I was born. I was cute. I learned to crawl. Pretty soon, I took my first step, then my second, then my third. I could walk across the living room. Then I started using the toilet." By now they don't dare glance at their reader's face, blanched white with disgust or worse yet, no face at all—out the door. Oops, they've lost their audience.

I'm afraid a lot of things we know no one really cares to hear about—the size of our shoes, how many times we urinate in a day, whether we put salt on our ham sandwich, the color of our favorite pen. The truth is, what we know matters less than how we tell it. We can't just lay everything out—the years of our life—one after the other—and think we have a book. The new writer quickly learns he needs something else, but the initial urge to write does seem to come from the heat of wanting to tell our story—what we know. We don't want to crush that energy. We need a form that unleashes our creative drive and also cuts through self-absorption and narrowness, breaking the writing, and our-selves, open.

First, we need to slow down and examine how memory works. I think of the line from the Chinese: "Old friend from far away," and I imagine a companion shrouded in mist I call to across mountains, the call echoing back. Who is this friend? Where can we find him? We discover that person is only within us. We carry his memory inside. Only there does your father live again and eat Bing cherries, watermelon and salami slices. Only you know how he swam laps alone summer after summer at Coney Island until he won the Brooklyn freestyle championship in 1933. At twenty his mother gave him a ruby ring that he never took off. Only you can still see the rubbed gem on his thick fist as he played poker at the kitchen table. As you bite into the heel of a pumpernickel loaf, you are awash with recollection. "Flooded with memories," we say. This propels us to write. The thoughts do not come in an orderly fashion. Memoir is connected to the way we remember. Writing memoir is another occasion to study the mind, to deepen our relation with that most potent writer's tool. But memoir is not sentimental; it does not cling. We write memoir to free ourselves. Those people we love have gone on, one way or another—through death or aging, a second marriage, a move to a new state. Why should we hold on any longer than they did? Here's your chance to make your father alive one last time on the page before you let him go. Don't forget the gray curl at the nape of his neck, the long, floppy earlobe, his gorilla walk, arms long and hairy, a step so far to the left he looks as though he'll topple, as though walking was a new discovery, even at eighty-three. What you do not write down will weigh down your father's jour-ney. He needs to go on, he wants to fly. Give him a new life of words and let them take off like electric birds.

Look at the beginning of *West with the Night* by Beryl Markham:

How is it possible to bring order out of memory? I should like to begin at the beginning, patiently, like a weaver at his loom. I should like to say, "This is the place to start; there can be no other."

But there are a hundred places to start for there are a hundred names—Mwanza, Serengetti, Nungwe, Molo, Nakuru. There are easily a hundred names, and I can begin best by choosing one of them—not because it is first nor of any importance in a wildly adventurous sense, but because here it happens to be, turned uppermost in my logbook. After all, I am no weaver. Weavers create. This is remembrance—revisitation; and names are keys that open corridors no longer fresh in the mind, but nonetheless familiar in the heart.

So the name shall be Nungwe—as good as any other—entered like this in the log, lending reality, if not order, to memory:

DATE—16/6/35
TYPE AIRCRAFT—Avro Avian
MARKINGS—VP–KAN
JOURNEY—Nairobi to Nungwe
TIME—3 hrs. 40 mins.

After that comes, PILOT: Self; and REMARKS—of which there were none.

But there might have been.

And off she goes for 293 pages. Did she capture everything? Of course not! She caught what came through her as she wrote. She allowed memory to inform the structure of her book. Memory and names, "Mwanza, Serengetti, Nungwe, Molo, Nakuru."

Try it for yourself. Name something you know even slightly. If you pay close attention, a whole card deck of thoughts begins to flip through your mind.

I write *Albert Lea* at the top of a notebook page:

Albert Lea was ninety miles south of Minneapolis. I'd drive in from the west on Highway 90, make a perfect right angle on 35W at Albert Lea and soon I'd be home for the six years I lived in Minnesota. Once in July I stopped in Albert Lea. I was hungry and walked its hot, humid streets. The glare from the shop windows stunned me into believing that even ninety miles was too far to drive, so I checked into a Super-8 at the edge of town. It was only one in the afternoon and I lolled around the rented room till five o'clock, flicking the TV on and off and then I jolted alive again. Suddenly I wanted to continue; I bolted from the motel, having paid for the night, and drove straight north like a sailing ship that caught the wind on the great Midwestern plains.

But this is a rough passage, the beginning of pulling out details, priming my recall. I'm hoping that the name will get me from a physical place to some emotional truth I wouldn't otherwise have located. When I re-read this note about one afternoon in Albert Lea, I recognize how lost and rootless I felt in my early thirties.

Now I'll try *Savannah River:*

Gray, and wider than the Rio Grande, in late February the river moved right outside my window the five days I spent in the city. I'd look up from the novel I was reading—the two main Indiana characters were going back and forth along the rows of corn with machinery I'd never heard of—and a black and enormous ship named the *Li Chin* chugged by my balcony. If I turned my head further north there was a graceful arched bridge that linked Georgia with South Carolina. At the end of my trip in a bakery on the riverfront I sent a succulent, golden pecan pie one morning to my friend Kate Green and her three boys up in St. Paul. I knew when Kate tasted the pie she'd feel the whole thing—the oaks hung with moss, the azaleas about to break open, the dogwood's delicate blossoms, the air thick and wet and the sluggish heavy Savannah I watched all week long.

I like these details about Savannah but what am I getting at? Details can give us a flavor, a sense of place, but that alone won't take me far enough in my writing. What's my relation to Kate that a pie I send her will let her experience the city I'm visiting? How are we both connected to the South? I'll eventually have to dig deeper, dive down through place and name into the dark riverbed, the currents that shape my life.

Sometimes I stretch my memory to beginnings and endings: a first kiss, then a last kiss; arriving in a place, leaving a place. To till the soil I try opposing assignments: I write everything I know about white for half an hour; then about black for the same amount of time.

I try to shake loose my mind, so something fresh can fall out. I tell myself to write about feeling fat, then go for ten minutes on how beautiful my mother was. I pause one moment only, then write on rain, then on Einstein, now Cinderella, another ten on a slow train, then a jaguar. It's like driving myself physically—run up this hill, then pedal your bike as fast as you can, dive into this fast-moving river and swim across, jump on the black horse on the other shore and gallop to town. When I exhaust myself, I let go. I'm willing to speak from a different place, to discover memories I didn't even know were there. This process acts like a sifter—sand falls through and bright nuggets come to light.

And all the while I try to stay connected to the senses: the hum of the refrigerator, the aroma of hot toast wafting in from the kitchen, burgundy sweater against her pale freckled skin, the velvet ridge of corduroy between my fingers, the broken taste of the apple that I ate as I cried. The senses make memory vivid. Often when I write I hear something far off, as if through a fog, and I go after that call in the dark.

Sense memories are a way to anchor us in the present and to open the past, to connect with it in a physical way, making it real and vivid. They help to cut through our "official story," the one we've made up about our lives and told over and over until we've created a shiny impenetrable veneer over the authentic truth. Often these manufactured stories are some kind of diagnosis—I was an alcoholic, I am an adult child, I am an incest survivor, I am a compulsive eater.

Stay away from labels. Move close to the dark aroma of whiskey, the flashing jukebox lights at your local tavern, the aching hunger you have inside, the crazy redhead with pale lipstick you fell for at the gas station and how she took every cent you had. Now the reader is hungry, too. She wants to come along with you. Take her. Don't let her smack up against a whitewashed facade.

We don't own our thoughts, even if they are filled with all our own details. They come through us, like heartbeat and breath. Allen Ginsberg said: "If the mind is shapely, then the writing will be shapely." First thoughts have their own structure, move in their own rhythm, rise full-muscled from the bottom of the mind. They appear and disappear, present themselves and fade away unless we try to smother them, frightened by their power and truth, or smash them into polite second or third thoughts. What might seem illogical—or scary—has its own integrity.

But all this reflection on our past can feel endless, shapeless, overwhelming. Where do we stop? This is where I rely on physical structure to shape infinity and give it form. My childhood went on forever, but I will pick only two pivotal times to write about: Part I, Natalie's Sixth Year; Part II, Her Twelfth Year. If I write deep enough into those two years, I'll get it all.

Think of the word: memoir. It's French. It's not an efficient, quick, sanitized prepackaged meal at McDonald's. It's a long afternoon, inhaling the bouquet of a rich port, sampling cheese, rolling a grape around in your mouth, a long conversation while another course is served, seeing light and shadow move across the street, long moments of silence. Suddenly I remember at the corner of my mind a friend from the hill country who ten years ago shot himself to death. I am surprised by the ache in my heart. I have time now to feel it, to sink into the whole experience of who he was, why he did it, what he meant to me.

For a long time I have emphasized detail with my writing students, but now it is time to pull out the structure behind the detail so we see the fabric that supports us. Who are we? How did we live? Names and details can be an anchor; but what we're ultimately looking for is below the surface. This deeper truth—the deep structure of our lives—is the key to writing memoir.

While I was working on *Long Quiet Highway,* a memoir about my Zen life, I dreamed that every morning I had to wake up at three AM, put on my rubber boots and wade in a cold, dark river, trying to grab eels with my bare hands. Awake, I was trying to write about my relationship with Katagiri Roshi, my teacher who died of cancer.

But the deep structure—what was it really all about, anyway, this New York Jewish woman meeting Japanese Zen master?—was slippery, like trying to catch inky fish in the middle of the night.

I knew I could not just introduce Roshi on page one; I was afraid American readers would shut the book after the first paragraph. In truth, I heard my grandmother's voice: "We came from Poland, worked hard for freedom, not for Natalie to become a slave with a master," or my father's incredulous reaction: "I fought the Japanese, now you study with them?" How could I bring my readers along with me? I began with my beloved ninth-grade teacher Mr. Clemente, who one stormy afternoon turned out the lights in the classroom and told us to listen to the rain. We've all had a treasured teacher in elementary or high school. I began with what was familiar. I took my reader's hand and slowly led him down the school corridor till finally on page one hundred we're standing at the front door about to meet the great teacher of my life—who also happened to be Japanese and a Buddhist.

Through that physical structure—how I set up the book—I got glimpses of the deeper structure of my life. My journey didn't begin when I met Katagiri; I'd consciously and unconsciously been looking for my teacher all my life. But don't think I truly understood that before I began to write.

Finding that inner structure is not easy. The search takes a certain faith and animal determination—a willingness to get to the core and expose ourselves. But often we honestly don't know how to find it. This is where work comes in, hard nerve and sweaty persistence: "I won't give up and I'll do whatever it takes."

At the publication party for his memoir *Truth Comes in Blows,* Ted Solotaroff told the story of how he wrote his book. Even though he is one of the great editors of his generation, he struggled for years with how to shape his own book. His research was prodigious. He wrote three hundred pages on the history of his family in Russia before they came to the United States. Then his editor at Norton read the huge first manuscript and said, "Ted, this book is really about you and your father."

Suddenly, the entire book came into focus. Solotaroff threw out the first three hundred pages and wrote an absolutely searing prologue about caring for his abusive father just before his death. Then he scrolled back to his childhood and began. The history of his family in Russia now takes up about four pages, told through the eyes of his family when he's a little boy.

Notice that Solotaroff took a cue—after his own great effort—from someone else. Don't always expect to get full understanding from yourself. There is a balance that we all have to learn: write, read what we have written, listen to ourselves, step away, talk to a few writing friends we trust, dive down again. And, like Solotaroff, we must be willing to throw a lot away, no matter how much hard work we've put into it. That work is not wasted. It's the path that leads to the entryway.

My friend Julie Landsman is the author of *Basic Needs, A Year with Street Kids in a City School* and two other memoirs, *Living with Men* and *White Teacher Talks About Race*. I asked her about her process. She studied with me for five years in the early eighties, so I was particularly curious to know how she moved from writing practice to creating books. Here's what she had to say.

First, she does straight writing practice. For example, in *Living with Men* she planned to examine her relationship with her father, her husband and her son. She began with her father and wrote everything she could think of, generating material using topics off a list she created. One of the topics was objects. She remembered that he'd always worn his Pensacola ring from the Naval Air station, where he did his pilot's training. As she described the ring, she suddenly saw the dining room light glint off the gold as he grabbed her when she came in the house after midnight smelling of Tim Carver's English Leather.

Once she had a collection of writing about her father, she let it sit while she went ahead and worked on the husband section. She said the longer she lets these first writing practices sit, the better—two weeks is good, a month is ideal.

When she finally read through the father material she was searching for themes—she doesn't know what they are ahead of time. This is important: she lets them emerge out of the actual work. No preconceived ideas. Of course, she has hunches, but she says they mostly prove to be false. Here she also checks what she is missing or hasn't covered.

Now, she says, she rearranges the original material by theme and hopes that an inner structure emerges. For example, fear of her father was one central motif that consistently flared up. He was such a tender man when he held her hand at a young age and walked around the Connecticut hills. In the evenings after work he bathed her in the big tub, using Johnson's shampoo, careful that her head was bent back as he rinsed the suds, then lifting her into a big warm blue towel that he wrapped around her young body. But then suddenly she was jarred by a later memory: he is in the kitchen, pacing back and forth, those same hands balled into fists—he did not like what she was telling him about the war in Vietnam. Julie realized he was good with small children; then her father was in control. He became angry as she grew older. He'd lost command—his daughter had her own mind.

Next she types directly from her handwritten notebooks what she has found and has underlined. (Yes, her original writing is by hand. She says it feels more physical and connected.) She prints out everything she has typed and lets it sit for a week.

After that Julie goes to a café she's never been to. She gets out of her studio in order to distance herself from the original process. When she reads now she's tough. She makes big cuts, not tiny edits, and she writes notes to herself—what needs to be added, remembering scenes she hasn't put in: "Write scene with Father in kitchen."

Only then does she actually begin to write her book: she slows down and enters, referring to her typed pages and notes. In order to keep the work vivid and alive, she goes back again to writing practice, but now with direction, purpose, always keeping in mind the inner structure in service now to something larger.

Next she gives what she's written to readers to get feedback. She chooses people she doesn't know too well, who won't be nice to her just because they're friends. She uses writers and nonwriters—two or three. More, she says, can get confusing. If her three readers know each other, she asks them not to discuss the manuscript with each other. Then, if all three say that something is too long, or that something else needs to be developed, she looks closely at it and makes her own decision. Otherwise, if everyone says something different, she usually stays with what she has.

After that she makes small revisions in sentence structure and individual words. Her critic doesn't really come in till this last stage, but even then she keeps her mind open, so that "I can be ready for important changes late in the process; for instance I suddenly remembered a tender moment with my father when I was older, and I realized that had to go in too."

Julie told me that each stage is fluid. She has presented the process as orderly—she does A, then B, then C—but sometimes as she's working on stage C, A slips in again. She may want to jolt her memory with some free writing or put C in front of A if she needs to ask a friend for feedback right at the beginning. Each stage uses a different state of mind and concentration: sometimes she's detailed; then loose, flooding the page; then receptive, re-reading her writing. She moves from one to another. Nothing is frozen.

Julie was teaching for thirty hours a week in the public schools while she wrote *Living with Men*. The first part of her process, generating material, took about a year. It took another two years to complete the book.

We were sitting in Café Con Amore in St. Paul on a brisk October day when she enumerated these steps to me. When she finished, I said, "Julie, I'm going to shoot myself! This is too much work." We laughed, both knowing I'm the Queen of Laziness, but as I drove around the Twin Cities all the rest of the day I realized what a clear, efficient approach Julie had developed.

My own method is more nebulous. Besides writing practice it includes days of walking, days when I never think of my writing. But deep in my belly, my inner compass is focusing due north, preparing. I use daydreaming, travel, meditation—always I'm hungry, waiting for the time I am ripe, feeding that place in me that wants to speak. I keep her silent until she glows red with anticipation and can't wait to discover herself on the page—then I charge like a wild animal onto the paper and pour it out. Later I re-read it with a silent prayer that I got it all down coherently the first time, that no rewriting is necessary. That's rarely true, but I am forever hopeful.

But after talking to Julie I wonder if I don't give too much of my energy and waking life to writing: I am always half where I am; the other half is feeding the furnace, kick-starting the heat of creativity. I am making love with someone but at the same time I'm noticing how this graceful hand across my belly might just fit in with the memory of lilacs in Albuquerque in 1974. I developed this approach when I was young and thought I had all the time in the world. Julie and I are older now. Writing is no longer the romantic activity it once was; there are books to be written. But I'll tell you a secret: Julie is the person in *Writing Down the Bones* who twenty years ago sat down on a hot, muggy afternoon in the small northern town of Hill City, Minnesota, on a wooden bench in front of the Rainbow Café, leaned back, stretched out her legs, and wrote in her notebook about her first sexual experience—and then her second, her third and so on. Night fell and she was still there, writing deep into her own sexual dream, the dark lake lapping at the shore a few hundred yards away.

THE INNER LIFE OF FICTION

EARLY ONE MARCH MORNING in 1993 John Thorndike, a writer friend, and I were moving a mattress from Santa Fe to Taos. As we drove along the narrow Rio Grande Gorge, the light just peeking over the Sangre de Cristos, John said, "OK, let's talk about *Banana Rose*. What's happening?"

Four months earlier, I'd received a four-page single-spaced letter from Linda Kahn, my fiction editor, suggesting changes on the first draft of my novel. In the preface as I'd written it, someone was cremated—but then was never mentioned again in the book. The preface was good, Linda said, it should stay, but something had to happen to connect it to the rest of the story. Someone was going to have to die.

Nailed! I thought when I read her letter.

Just before I'd mailed Linda the manuscript, I'd called another writer friend, Cecil Dawkins, down in Santa Fe. "Cecil, are you allowed to have a preface that has nothing to do with the book?"

"Honey," she drawled (Cecil is from Alabama), "you're allowed anything you want." She paused, "As long as it works."

I guessed my preface didn't work. I froze after I read that letter from Linda. Now, so many months later, John was trying to cajole me to open up.

I looked out the passenger window at the almost white, early spring river, then I looked down at my boots. I heard a little voice in me say, go ahead, try it, tell John. I mustered my courage: "Well, what do you think if Anna is the one to somehow die?" I uttered something that had been at the periphery of my perception for months, but it was scary for me and I'd continued to push it away. After all, what did I really know about writing a novel? This was my first, and I loved Anna. I didn't want her to die.

I glanced over at John. He was lit up. "Yes, that's it," he said, unequivocally. "And the cremation scene could appear again in different details at the end of the book."

John never gave in so easily. He usually played devil's advocate. Often we yelled at each other over my kitchen table. He liked to chew up a manuscript. And here he was immediately surrendering to my idea.

Two weeks later I was in New York face-to-face with Linda and Toni Burbank, my nonfiction editor. John's response gave me the courage to tell them what I had told him. We were sitting in a small conference room twenty-five floors above the swarming streets of Manhattan.

I took a breath—these were seasoned editors—and I spoke. "I thought Anna should die at the end. She should be cremated." Toni's face lit up with the same acknowledgment that John's had and tears sprang into Linda's eyes.

At that moment I realized with certainty that writing fiction was not some flim-flam operation——Hey, I can make up whatever I want! I knew that in memoir the writer was anchored in reality, but when I switched to fiction, I thought imagination would let me do anything. Now I saw that fiction had to conform to or mirror an inner rightness or structure that we carry within our psyches. One of the reasons we read a story is to bring forth from within ourselves that glow, that *yes*. The tale affirms something large within us. The structure of *Banana Rose* had become bigger than my little will. Anna was no longer mine. She had stepped into the life of fiction, and karmic determination, or plot, took over. She had to die no matter how unfair it seemed to me, no matter how wonderful she was. The truth of the story was deeper than my love or desire for things to be different.

Recently I read *South of the Big Four* by Don Kurtz. Arthur, the main character, was having an extramarital affair with Annie, a café waitress. I was a cheerleader as I read, rooting for the characters to do the right thing——not morally, but to live up to what I knew to be true in these situations and true to the characters Kurtz had created. Yes, that's right, I'd say to myself, she'd do that in the Holiday Inn. Uh-oh, I'm not sure now, they haven't seen each other in three weeks, would they immediately go to bed? Did the author lose it? OK, now, after lovemaking they quarrel for a while——they have to get used to each other again. Yes, that's right, I sighed, relieved. Annie's been busy with her husband and four kids. She's not sure of Arthur. She has to feel proof of his caring. I was monitoring the truth of Kurtz's writing, watching how close he stayed to the marrow of human relationship.

At each new turn of events I held my breath: could Kurtz pull it off? And when he did, I exhaled with relief. I felt that rush, that joy of connection. All's right with the world. Now this doesn't mean all's good, fair, just. Just true to the underlying structure of life.

Once in a lecture, my Zen teacher Katagiri Roshi said, "There are sixty-five instants in a moment."

Interrupting his talk, I rudely blurted out, "Hold everything! Where'd that come from? How do you know that?"

"Monks in caves. They sat steadily for thirty years. Their minds were so slowed down they could watch the instants arise and count them." He nodded in encouragement.

"Oh," I said. That alone quieted me—they slowed down that much?

One of the things those monks probably saw was that nothing stops. Even at a vastly slower pace, birth and death are rising and falling, rising and falling, like our breath. One of us may die, but someone's breath goes on breathing. If we all die, the trees will continue. If an atom bomb drops, it stops this earth, but that's just our great, small daub of paint on the vast palette of the rising, falling universe. So our individual thoughts might stop, but the structure of the cosmos continues.

How can this help us in writing? Don't get caught and tied up in the mosquito net of desire and will. Trust the design holding up the netting. Move quickly. Don't think and plot too much. Surrender to the structure of the mind and it will give you much more freedom. We don't know where we're going: trust the rise and fall.

We can set up parameters: our character is twenty-two, selling flowers on a London street corner in chapter one. We know where we're heading: in the last chapter he will die on a Friday in the rain in Los Angeles. OK, now navigate the story as though it were a ship in deep water, a whale in the ocean currents, a dream under our sleep.

Suzuki Roshi once said to his sixties American students that the way they dressed—with beads, long hair, brightly colored clothes—they all looked alike. Shave your heads, wear black robes, he said—Ah, now I can see your uniqueness.

Our ideas and intentions can mask and cover up a story; there is a life force that will declare itself if you let it. Get out of the way.

EAT THE MOUNTAIN

TWO YEARS AGO near the end of a workshop a student burst out: "Why, writing is the new religion!" I laughed, but I knew what she meant. In our secular society, usually suspicious of traditional forms of spirituality, writing is a place where we can meet ourselves deeply, encounter the imprint of something immense running through us. It's a place to face wild mind head-on and to apprehend the design of the universe.

Last week I ran into a friend who knew another friend. I asked about him. "Oh, he's great. He's working on a book that he feels is his life's work," she said. He was a poet and I immediately assumed he was assembling his collected works. She continued: "He's writing a book about how to write poetry."

What? When I heard that I realized many people now are more interested in the process or *way* of a writer than in any writer's individual work. Perhaps I shouldn't be surprised. After all, didn't I do that, too? But I thought I was an anomaly. I see now that there's an entire movement. When *Writing Down the Bones* came out in 1986, bookstores put it in the reference section. Now, at the end of our millennium, they have separate sections dedicated to books on writing. I run my finger along their spines: how to write a novel in your spare time, how to be your own agent. How to let your dreams write your books, how your inner child can help your poetry. I think the secret yearning here is, how do we encounter our own minds? We are searching for the core of our lives; our culture intuits that writing, that ancient activity, might be a pathway.

A writer's path includes concentration, slowing down, commitment, awareness, loneliness, faith, a breakdown of ordinary perceptions—the same qualities attributed to monks or Zen masters. Writers practice for literature and for the illusory victory of publication, while monks prepare for enlightenment, which is nothing less than ego's great disappointment. Awakening does not feed ego's needs and desires; it pulverizes the self. Our society couldn't knowingly bear such reduction, so we've tricked ourselves into the same path but call it writing. We are less and less interested in its products and more interested in its process—the way monks come to understand that there is only the emptiness of nothing permanent or solid, nothing to hold on to in the end.

But the way we learn is never as clear as a neat, guided walk through a California nature preserve. In fact, the idea of a path, getting from one place to another, is probably an illusion. Mostly there is a process of unfolding. At the end a spiritual person turns around and sees the design of her life and calls it a path. This most likely can also be said for a writer's life. There isn't any clear passage.

This is true for the writing of most books, too. The book's shape is often evident only after a writer has almost finished—it develops like a photo under water in the dark. But does this contradict what I said earlier, that I couldn't write *Writing Down the Bones* before I had a structure for it? At the time, book structure was not internal for me. I needed a vision of some architecture in order to write the book. But as a writer continues, I think, structure becomes more internal and the writer naturally speaks in the genre's form.

When I started writing poetry, I was awkward, clumsy. I wasn't sure how to put my thoughts and images into poems. I wanted to show friends what I wrote and ask not, "Do you like it?," but "Is this really a poem—these broken lines with eggs, boots and whistling all thrown together? Does it add up to something or am I a fool?" It was like swimming out into a big body of water, into the Atlantic Ocean, and claiming a hunk of that water as mine, concentrated and colored with my mind. As I continued to swim and become saturated, I comprehended the form and instinctively wrote in the contour of poetry. I figured out how to pour my share of water into a bowl, a cup, bottle, even a bathtub. I learned by practice and also by reading and listening to a lot of poems. I began to internalize the structure of poetry so that when I spoke on paper my words came out as a poem. This does not mean all poems have the same form; but there is some essence that distinguishes a poem from an automobile engine manual. By continued work I incorporated that essence.

When I began to write prose I had to embrace a whole new mode of construction. After poetry, prose felt like laying bricks. One sentence after another. No fanciful leaps where I could presume the reader was following me. Subject, verb, direct object. I had to stretch my line. I felt encumbered, not like the flight I knew with poetry. But soaring came with prose, too, as I slowly learned to navigate its waters.

Now that I write books, I imagine myself as a builder constructing houses. I build a split-level like the one I grew up in on Long Island—three bedrooms, two baths, a garage, a kitchen, sunken living room, den. That's one book. Then I move to Huntington, a town in Suffolk County: I decide to add a patio and eliminate the garage.

Book two. But then I'm tired of split-levels and in Cold Spring Harbor I build a ranch house. Book three gets completed. I find that none of the buildings get easier, even though I've become more experienced in my profession. In Bay Shore township they have different zoning requirements and it turns out the land I have to build on is two-thirds sand and the building demands a basement. And then in Bethpage the well won't run clear. Each place I build, the territory is unique.

Finally, I become sick of suburbia altogether and flee to the West. I decide to experiment with solar houses built into the earth, but I miscalculate the water table and the walls start collapsing.

You say, it serves you right. Quit moving around so much—settle down.

But, I reply, the nature of building—of creativity—is to clear land and construct.

Each new book I attempt is more difficult. When I was young, the mountain seemed far away. I had a lot of energy to run to it and lots of new things to say. But now I have arrived at the mountain and my body's pressed against it. I've said everything I know; I have to go to the unknown to speak. With no space between me and the mountain I have to move this mammoth escarpment each time— even one centimeter—to produce a book. The mountain's heavy, huge; my body's tired, getting older. All this I didn't know in my early, loving flush with writing.

But still there is the hope we become a little more intelligent. One way to move the mountain is to eat it, take bites out of it. Then at least the power of its structure is inside us and we become more of a match for it.

Two summers ago I read *Crossing to Safety* by Wallace Stegner. I'd never read a novel of his before. I was astounded by his agility, his freedom in that form. It seemed he could do whatever he wanted and it worked. I felt broken open to the possibilities of fiction. Everything in his story has come together, it's gaining momentum near the end and I am greedily bearing down the track, when suddenly, in a segue that almost gives me whiplash, Stegner takes the characters to Venice for a year. I thought, you can't do that! But that scene in Italy—they stand on their apartment balcony and look out on the soft, filtered light of this romantic city—creates a sudden opening, a kind of grace just before the terrible fate that awaits the characters back across the sea.

After I read that novel I walked around the streets of Taos stunned for three sizzling summer months. Stegner never flinched, but stayed in the fire's heat of his creation. I bought the book for friends, then nagged them to read it, eager to share lunch and talk about it. I was obsessed. How did he do it?

What I didn't realize then was that this novel was his last, written near the end of his life. Six years after its publication, when he was eighty-four, he came to Santa Fe to receive an award from the Mountains and Plains Booksellers for his latest book of essays. As he drove to his hotel after the banquet, his car was broadsided. Wallace Stegner—this great and esteemed writer—died of internal injuries in the oldest city in the West.

By the time Stegner wrote *Crossing,* the design of a novel was his—he'd earned it. He'd probably eaten a good portion of the mountain by then, and he was free to take it where he wanted. But this doesn't mean his last novel was easy to write. Free and easy are two different things.

SHALL WE PLOT ALONG?

WHEN I MET KATE GREEN, late in the morning on a hot August day in 1978, she was twenty-seven years old, and it seemed she'd been a poet all her life. She told stories about studying with Anne Sexton at Boston University: how Sexton lit one cigarette while she still had another half smoked, hanging from her mouth; how she told the class not to try to impress her with their knowledge of literature—she wouldn't know what they were talking about, she hadn't gone to college. How late one Wednesday afternoon a small group of women from Sexton's class picked her up from the airport and they went to a bar. After a few drinks Sexton said to them, "You can't be afraid to be a fool and if you're not willing to be a fool, get out of this business right now." How two days later Kate heard over radio static that Anne Sexton, the Pulitzer Prize-winning poet, had killed herself.

When I first encountered Kate, she had just completed her first novel. She had worked on it for three years. It opened with Sadie Kansas riding on a train, looking out the window. Sadie's mind wandered on the first page, and that was it. Her mind kept going, never to return to the train, to the plastic upholstery, to the handles at the corners of seat backs to grab as the train rolls and jolts as you walk down the aisle, or to the windows, looking out on mountains, plains, the rain, the dust and sand blown up in wind, the leaning trees, the barn, the kids getting off a yellow school bus. None of it.

Years later, Kate told me, "I was a poet trying to write a novel and it was a five-hundred-page single-spaced prose poem with no time structure, no point of view, no dramatization and nothing happening! Naturally it was all based on my own life so I thought it was interesting, but all it was was confusing."

She called it a complete failure and then she softened a bit and called it her "training wheels novel."

After that blunder she set out to study plot, to give herself guidelines.

Well, I can hear a student ask, why didn't someone tell her earlier? Then she wouldn't have wasted three years.

Someone should also have told us before we got married that we would get divorced. Someone should have warned us that our leg would break, so we wouldn't go skiing. Writing one novel carries us to the next. We enter the water and swim. Writing, I'm afraid, is not as safe and sure-fire as we'd like it to be. Kate's second novel, *Shattered Moon,* however, was nominated for an Edgar Allan Poe Award, a major prize for mystery writers.

Shattered Moon started from one idea, from a flash: a psychic would foresee her death and then try to change or avoid that death. Kate saw that the idea lent itself to a mystery form. Since plot was her short suit, she knew she'd have to put it right up front and pay attention to it the way a painter might study color or a dancer work on leaping or a trumpet player concentrate on a kind of breathing or blowing.

She decided the novel would have thirty chapters; there had to be action in each chapter, and she would set it up so that when readers came to the end of a chapter, they'd want to go on to the next.

Does this sound too mechanical? Listen to what Kate told me about how she filled in this framework:

I had to lie down for two months during my first pregnancy and so I decided I would just journal about this idea and see where it took me. This is still the way I work. I just free write about the story and the plot and the characters and I have dreams about the story and I talk it over with people and just keep writing all of that down, free writing as I go. I get an idea for a scene or an event that could happen. Then I think, if this happens, then this will have to happen in the past to get ready for this. So I go for months, usually three months to a year. The more steadily I write (as in writing practice), the more alive the story becomes for me. It is electricity in my creativity, lots of ideas flying around and through. I don't try to have it make sense. It is a very right-brained associative activity. I am not working chronologically at all, like first what would happen in chapter one, then in two. I just am all over the terrain of the story. It is changing as I think of things. There are many possibilities and alternatives, seven different ways to end, ten possible places to begin. It is mercurial. It is just basically notes for a possible story.

As I run into things that I don't have information on, I do research. I read about movie production and direction; talk to owners of auto-body shops about bullets going through different kinds of glass; hang out in a billiard hall and talk to people to get ideas for characters; meet with the FBI, the

Minnesota Bureau of Criminal Apprehension, the Marin County Coast Guard, Italian fishermen off the coast of Drake's Bay in northern California; study with psychics; talk to a psychiatrist at the Mayo Clinic, and travel to the place where the book will be set. I do this when I'm journaling before I begin and all throughout the book whenever I need information or energy.

Finally, in this writing practice notebook, I get to a place where I can sense that I can begin. I have pretty much converged on a story line and can tell that any more journaling is just spinning my wheels and it is time to leap into the actual writing. This is a pretty hard transition to make and requires some avoidance and resistance on my part. Finally, I just make a writing practice schedule and begin.

I wrote my first novel teaching elementary school and writing at a little desk in the school library for about thirty-five minutes a day on my lunch hour. When summer came I hired a baby-sitter from nine to noon four days a week and finished it. I have to remind myself of this now because I'm teaching full time and am a single mom of three sons and feel sorry for myself feeling that I have no time to write. Time to write is simply that. An hour here, a half an hour there. Go. Move pen. That's it. The rest is all bullshit and I know it but I get caught up in it and create a lot of suffering around not writing. Writing itself is pretty simple. "Just do it."

Kate has since published four more novels, a series of children's stories and two books of poetry. Recently I told her I'd take her out to a great restaurant if she told me everything she knew about plot while we ate dinner. Though the food turned out to be lukewarm and self-conscious (a bum tip on a St. Paul bistro) Kate was hot, eager to talk about writing again. Her father had recently died. They were close and he had given her her running orders: write well and make money. OK, Dad, I could hear her whisper to him, as she leaned over the small table to talk with me.

"Plot is what happens, Nat. A woman sitting and having a cup of tea is good for one sentence. Plot is a sequence of actions that compels a reader to want to know more. It's a seduction, bread crumbs dropped deeper and deeper into the woods—into the unknown."

She later said that it is the structure of the actions that makes a reader turn the page. A journal might have a series of actions—I went to the store; I said hi to Frank; I drove home—but it doesn't compel a reader. Our lives appear to move chronologically: this, then this, then this, so we think story moves that way, too. But plot can go backward, break into dialogue, reminisce. Suddenly there's a place description, information can be given, or a long love scene can happen.

I stopped her here: "You know, Kate, that's really how our lives move, too. It's an illusion that we progress. Instead our lives wander into a store, then into a thought, then into a desire like 'I'm thirsty.' "

Just then a waitress handed us the dessert menu. I can't remember what was on it. Hay with whipped cream, boiled barley, nuts and shredded chocolate? I tried to recall who had recommended this place. We wrinkled our noses. No, neither of us would have dessert.

"Yes," Kate said, pulling me back from thoughts of cheesecake. "And I think the best stories are the ones where all the elements are not separated but woven together—the character, the place and so on. Then plot is more than just an action that happens. The action reveals character, it's anchored in a setting, it reverberates in memory. It's not separate, like, 'OK, here is a big action now, watch closely.'

"This is what a good plot feels like," Kate murmured. I leaned in, hungry. "You don't want to skip ahead. Everything feels germane. You are afraid you'll miss something important. You want to keep reading. You plan to go to bed early so you'll have more time with the book. You stay up too late. You are as changed by the story as the characters are."

She paused. More, more. I still wanted a lot of dessert.

"It is what happens. It better be good, it better matter, it better not trail off or give up or wimp out. It better lodge in the heart. It better take up residence and live on in the hearer, the listener, the reader. It better be a living transmission."

We started to laugh. She slapped the table. "Now get to work."

I remembered the day so many years ago when Kate introduced me to cornfields in northern Minnesota. The stalks were already high. She was pregnant with her first son. We pulled the car over and walked down the long rows till there was nothing else but tassels and green shafts. I turned to her—she was chewing gum and I was munching on a Kit-Kat. "Will we always be happy—and write?"

"Of course," she replied.

Kate and I had so many dreams and plans that day in the cornfields. But how do things unfold? You do something and something results. Kate and I couldn't really know where our lives were going. And besides, don't most of us keep revising our stories as we go along? One year we think we should have stayed married, he was the deep love of our life. The next year we think we were fools and he was a damn bastard. Our human lives seem to unravel—there's no apparent plan. But a fiction plot illustrates the universal structural law of karma. You do something and there is a result. Plot is the direction, the core we only see—if we're lucky—when we turn around and look back years later.

Sometimes plot is a fast train running down a straight track; other times it's a fat pear rolling off our open palm. If we don't know where we're going in our lives and if the characters don't know, that's OK, as long as the author knows where he's taking us—even if he's only taking us to where the pear plops down at our feet, to a place where we already are.

Deep in the matrix of the human mind is a desire to find out what is going to happen; even more, what the meaning of this is: what is our life all about? An author hooks into that structure in the mind and pulls us along—how will these characters turn out?

Years before Bantam bought *Banana Rose,* I sent an early version to my editor, Toni Burbank, and asked her to read it. Then I went to New York. We sat in her office. I'm sure she had some nice things to say about the manuscript, but I already knew that with editors, you have to wait for the "but." I was holding my breath. This time it was, "But Natalie, it has no narrative drive." I nodded dutifully as though I understood. What was she talking about? I had no idea, but I acted as though I did. After all, this was my New York editor. I didn't want to look like a complete fool. Hadn't I just a half hour earlier rushed into Saks across the street to buy chic pointy black leather shoes and shoved my hiking boots—still crusty with Taos dirt—into my bulky purse? And now if I wasn't going to be uncool with my clunky combat footwear, I certainly wasn't going to display my ignorance about those two words, though I made powerful note of them in my mind: *narrative drive.*

As soon as I returned home I called Kate Green long distance for an explanation. "Don't be ridiculous. You know what it is," she replied.

"But I don't," I whined. I couldn't convince her. She couldn't believe her brilliant friend wouldn't know something so fundamental.

The truth is I was ignorant, and I needed time to slowly absorb and understand how stories work. From teaching I've discovered many other people don't understand either. Narrative drive is simple but important; Mrs. Post should have taught us about it. Bluntly put: it's what propels us to turn the page. I think I discovered the explanation in a style book, but I only knew it over time as it fell through my whole body, so when I began serious revisions a year later I hit the page running.

Then I saw that although lots happened in *Banana Rose,* one incident didn't propel the reader into the next. I had to make things connect, not just paint one picture, then another. My job was to grab my reader's hand and move her along, hook into her longing for meaning—what's next, what will happen to Nell now that she did this, then this. There had to be forward motion.

I realized there is a reason cars are not equipped to go backward for long distances. We all have an impulse to go ahead, even if we drive right down a dark alley to a dead-end street where, we've been warned, someone has been lynched. We jam on the brakes, look up at the swinging body; the corpse has our face.

But, of course, we also need to be interested in the novel's character to get in the car in the first place. If he's a real dud, we won't care what happens to him. The author will lose us no matter how many action firecrackers he tries to explode. If we like or identify with the character, we just might go a piece with her even if she's just bumbling down the side of the road.

SHE HAD TO LOVE CHOCOLATE

WHEN I BEGAN *BANANA ROSE* I wanted to write my great life story. And, naturally, I thought I'd structure the main character after darling Natalie at twenty-six. I'd substitute a four-letter name, N-E-L-L, for the usual seven, keep the initial *N* as a hint for cagey readers, and otherwise, follow along with everything that had happened to me. It seemed simple enough. What was all this moaning about fiction being difficult?

But here was my big mistake: I created Nell by subtracting elements from my own character. I knew I couldn't put in everything, so I selected certain traits. She had to love chocolate and sweets; she was afraid of some things, brazen about others; had strong opinions, a New York accent; was sensuous and had brown eyes. I made her hair curly—mine was straight—another cagey move. In some ways, I think I made a cartoon of myself; I reduced Nell to gestures and desires.

No book can ever capture a flesh-and-blood human being exactly as she is. We're all too complicated, too quirky, too uncontrollable. And we don't know ourselves as well as we'd like to think. My understanding of myself is always changing, my image moves like a kaleidoscope. One week I'm struck by my need to travel more and live in foreign countries; the next I begin to type up a résumé, I'm going to apply for a Ph.D. in literature. A month later I settle down into cooking—I want to learn the best chicken recipes. Who am I anyway?

No, I couldn't have captured it all, but I had unknowingly left out the one thing that gives me, and would have given Nell, a motor, a reason for being on this earth. In the original manuscript Nell did nothing. She was a hippie, she hung out.

Linda, *Banana Rose*'s editor, said, "It's boring; people don't do nothing."

"We did back then," I told her brightly.

I thought, what a pipsqueak Linda is. She's only in her twenties. What does she know of my great generation, the late sixties kids? We didn't have worldly ambitions. We wanted to see the light, come face-to-face with truth. Peace, not war, we shouted.

"It doesn't make good reading. Have her do something."

"OK," I swallowed.

When I was twenty-six what I wanted most was to become a writer. I filled notebooks with my thoughts, descriptions, stories. But I never thought of making Nell a writer, I wasn't even aware how central that drive was to my own human character. Take that force away and Nell was charming but not compelling. Do I dare say, she was a bit of a dud?

Since then, I've discovered that other first novelists have made this mistake, too. My friend Eddie and I have discussed this over many hamburgers and layer cakes. His main character in *Ray Had an Idea About Love* had many lovable—and not-so-lovable—qualities. We knew Ray was looking for love and self-understanding after his divorce (so was Eddie), and that he was an electrician (like Eddie).

But Eddie left out the passion that makes him one of my best friends: he majored in English literature at Harvard and burns to write fiction, and he writes even though he has a demanding job and is raising two kids. He eliminated a key complexity of his human life, one that makes him interesting and unique—that driving creative appetite that has the capacity to destroy anything in its way.

How do we miss something so obvious? First, we are not so obvious to ourselves. Writers have a dumb naïveté. It had taken me a long time to give writing a place in my life. I remember hearing my mother's advice, "Dear, why don't you get a teaching certificate? You can write in the summers." I was half-ashamed of how much I loved reading, how I could enter worlds of my imagination, daydream at the drop of a hat, be curious about a past thunderstorm, a dead raven, a divorce that everyone else told me to forget. Why should I step forth and expose my character to humiliation? I wanted to keep her safe, not to unveil in Nell my deepest yearning. I was finally in control. Nell would be a sweet love child watching the world go by. I was willing to make her a bit irascible but not to reveal her lean hunger, her fierce desire for self-expression and her desperation, her demands on life. No. No. No.

But here's the catch: people don't really like to read about nice people. What is the first line of Tolstoy's *Anna Karenina*? "Happy families are all alike." We want to read about cruel impulses, raw desire—we want the author to get down and to take us there.

My protection of Nell wasn't obvious to me, but after Linda's comment, I made Nell a painter. A writer felt too obvious—don't forget, I was trying to be cagey. In fact, I had been painting all those years, too, but I never thought to really notice it. I took my underbelly, my own unconscious activity, and stepped forward with it in Nell. These motivations weren't clear to me. I was struggling to make this damn novel work and grabbing what I could. "Get Nell active," Linda said and I tried to trust her suggestion—maybe she knew something.

I tend to go into things blind, and when I'm kicked down I get up. That's my practice. I enter the dark canal and hope for birth. I am a fool—I had no idea how hard a novel was to write. Now it was demanding courage of me. I couldn't hide behind my tintype characters, I had to give them muscle. I had to hand over my life force to them, show my real raw self, not just the self I'd like everyone to believe in. I had to wake people up with the truth. Oh, my god. Here I go.

But here is the other catch. Once I'd given my characters guts and will, I found that none of them wanted to go where I directed them. I wanted to cling to what I knew—this was my story! Not only was Nell me, but the others in the novel were my friends in those days. But the truth was, it was stifling to try to capture what I thought had happened. I needed to shed the weight of my own life. For a year and a half I struggled to govern every move my characters made, and I was miserable. I did timed writing practices and pretended my stories and characters were made up. I knew Kate Green did free-writing portraits to get to know her people, to reinvent them over and over. She'd write their dreams, their motivations. But oh, no, not me. I didn't know what I was doing and I don't think I wanted to know. Nell was too close to my life—who wanted to be conscious of that?—the reader could read the book later and figure out who I was. I wasn't secure enough in writing fiction. I was afraid if I stopped a moment to think, I'd quit the whole project. I knew there was no Nell—it was only me. This could be a terrible failure, I thought every day when I was done. But, just as a miner who is digging for gold can't think this might be the wrong plot of land, I plowed that shovel into the plot day after day.

I made believe I was Nell telling Nell's story. And then one day, lo and behold! It was early spring, March, I had on a gray crewneck sweater. Outside the café window snow was lightly dusting Taos Plaza, the lighting was poor over the wood table, my left hand held a brown mug of lukewarm mint tea, and as I wrote, Natalie faded out. She was gone, disappeared, and this character Nell Schwartz was telling her own story through my hand. I was no longer doing writing practice. Nell was doing writing practice, telling all about her adventures, her boyfriend, her girlfriends, her home, her parents, her sister. Even now I can remember the sensation of feeling unglued—I experienced a heady freedom. I no longer existed. I could lay down my burden and let the kid walk on her own two feet.

Then one morning as I wrote, Anna appeared. Nell was walking the rim in Valdes and this tall, rather gangling young woman was coming toward her from the opposite direction. The important thing was: I let it happen. I surrendered. I finally didn't recoil or try to control the writing. I let her meet Nell; I described her hair, her eyes, the shape of her face. That improbable element, Anna, a person who did not exist in my autobiographical life, split the whole novel apart. Her presence opened the true path of the story.

But she wasn't real? my students ask.

Well, she was partially taken from a deep old friend, Barbara Schmitz from Norfolk, Nebraska.

And isn't it true that our psyches merge and incorporate everyone we encounter anyway? The people we befriend usually mirror ourselves, our known and unknown parts. Those friends are in us. And now they were trotting into my novel. But we shouldn't worry: no one is holding up over our shoulder the true map of our life—"Uh-uh, Nat, I see from my diagram that there was no Anna." No one cares that much. Readers only want to be engaged. Pull them in.

And there was an Anna! She appeared on the page and as I let go I realized that Anna and Nell were two parts of my psyche having a dialogue. One was a fiery Jew; the other was a deep, slow Midwesterner. I got to play them out on the page.

When a friend asked, how did you ever think of making Anna's eye go cockeyed? I smiled coyly, as if it was just another one of my brilliant ideas. In truth, I have loved Carson McCullers faithfully and fiercely ever since I read *The Ballad of the Sad Café* in ninth grade. The main character, Miss Amelia with her odd eyes, has loomed large and clear in my imagination. When Anna wasn't derived from an old friend or myself, I borrowed elements from Miss Amelia. At forty-two when I created Anna, McCullers's character was deeply embedded in my consciousness. I'd read the book at least ten times and mused on Miss Amelia's love predicament often when I took long walks in the hills. Anna was partly a tribute to *Ballad of the Sad Café* and my deep pleasure in Carson McCullers's writing. No one I know has made that connection, but I gave everyone a hint. When Nell first meets Anna she has that novel stuffed in her back pocket.

But are you allowed to do that—I can hear a student ask—to take an element of someone else's character?

Sure I can. It's the way I planted my book in the lineage of fiction and paid homage to one of its finest writers.

After the novel was published, people asked me: "How come Nell's not fat?"

"Huh, what do you mean?"

"She's always eating." Unbeknownst to me, in almost every chapter there was food. I remember Toni Burbank saying to me at one point, get her to do something else; and I said to myself, what else? That's ridiculous. You've got to eat. You meet a friend—and eat. You think of making love—and eat. You go for a hike—and stuff your backpack with food. But I certainly wasn't aware just how much she was eating. Now I realize that Nell used the structure of meals as a way to ground each writing. Once she was present, she could go on to other things. Doesn't food work this way for all of us? The smell of lasagna in the oven, the taste of an orange, marmalade on hot toast, the weight of blueberries in our hand—we're right there, we can count on it. When I feel anchored, I write clearly. Nell used eating as a mooring device, a position or foundation from which to tell her story.

But the scariest question for all aspiring writers, who want to write about their lives and loves, inevitably lifts its formidable head at almost all writing workshops I teach: what about your ex-husband! Won't he sue you? And your mother, your friends, won't they be mad at how you depicted them?

Yes, I was worried about my ex-husband. He's a fine man. We still have a deep connection, though we're seldom in contact. I was nervous—maybe he'd hate me, even take legal action. That specter hung over me, especially at the beginning, when I was shaky about the whole undertaking. And I'd have to say the dread kept up like a fine thread humming through the whole nine years until the novel was finally out. (That many years? Yes, it took three years to write the first draft, and then I put it away for three years after I received my first feedback.) I'd read about it in the newspaper, see it on TV, how an irate husband won his case in court and was now receiving fifty percent of the royalties! I'd feel a bitter taste in my mouth— let him write his own story if he wants to make money. Finally, I had to put my concerns aside. For a while, I tried to make every-thing nice, so no one would be offended. I was back in Mrs. Post's class. The words slid right off the page. No clout, no texture, no rough edges. More like three-day-old warmed-over bean soup.

I realized I had to ride the ruddy edges of my truth, and that's what it was: *my truth*. Not my ex-husband's, not my mother's. The story wouldn't happen if I kept others' feelings foremost in my mind. Plus who knew if it would even get published? These fears kept me from writing. Not good. I had to put them aside when I was actually doing the work. I could pick them up afterward to torture myself.

As the novel developed, I left the actual occurrences way behind anyway. My father-in-law never rode a horse up to Blue's house to serenade her (I wasn't even sure he could ride a bike). My mother, in the guise of Nell's mother, never got caught in an outhouse with her pants down. (Though once she did visit me and stand outside one; she said it smelled terrible.) As I became more confident, I found that fiction allowed me to move into a fourth dimension, out to universes that never actually occurred but might have. I began to step off the edge, leap off the pole, jump from the bridge.

Milan Kundera in his novel *The Unbearable Lightness of Being* says that characters in his novels are his own unrealized possibilities. "That is why I am equally fond of them all and equally horrified by them. Each one has crossed a border that I myself have circumvented. It is that crossed border (the border beyond which my own 'I' ends) which attracts me most."

Who could we be in the peripheral vision of our life? A hobo? We fear this possibility: someday despite our best efforts it will all fall apart and we will be penniless. As a writer we can go for it— develop that tramp, give him a face, hands, his lost life. I chose people I knew and then took them out beyond where they'd been, but not beyond what my imagination could sustain. If in life a friend was a mathematician, it seemed too great a leap to dream him into a famous actor. I tried at first to create characters only one degree different from myself or a friend. A mathematician could become an accountant or an engineer, or maybe a math teacher with a limp.

Often when I ask students to list their unrealized potentials, they create characters too fantastical, as though a romance novelist or Hollywood producer had made them up: astronaut, Olympic triathlete, beauty queen, rock star, famous movie actor. Beyond a few glitzy details, most of us don't know enough of the inner workings of these people to sustain us for long. As we progress, our ability to project ourselves increases, but at the beginning it's a good idea to stay close to home. This doesn't mean that if you live on Flatbush Avenue in Brooklyn, your character has to be around the corner, but a cowboy in Montana seems a bit far-fetched. Try it if you must, but beware—he'll probably have a Brooklyn heart. Whoever you write about will be close to home whether you like it or not. Don't ever think you can run away.

In *Banana Rose* I gave the hippie name Gauguin to the main male character, who was inevitably modeled on my ex-husband Neil. I made Gauguin an expert horseman, though Neil knew nothing about horses. I love horses, but I am afraid of them. I'd never dared even to stroke one on the neck. But for the novel I took horseback-riding lessons. I learned how to clean around their shoes, comb and saddle them. I listened intently to detailed descriptions of my friends' riding episodes. As soon as I wrote the horse scenes, I quit the lessons. Those horses were huge. They could crush me. Better to ride my mind.

I had Gauguin ride horses because it helped to break open the character, to separate him from the person I knew. When Gauguin, as a young boy, rode out in the Iowa hills in moonlight and laid his head back on the horse's rump while staring up at the starry night, I was able to convey a sense of my character's dreaminess. Of course I could have had him simply daydream out his classroom window in fourth grade, but it didn't feel as intimate. Gauguin was a romantic character for me. I knew classrooms. They weren't romantic enough.

About six months after *Banana Rose* was published, I received an early Saturday-morning phone call from my ex-husband. "Nat, I just finished your novel."

I swallowed and sat down at the kitchen table.

"I had no idea you were so blown out by our break-up."

In all the years I was writing I had never imagined this response. We had a good long talk—probably the best and deepest since our divorce many years ago. He said it was fascinating to see what I'd done with those times, the way I'd experienced things.

I learned I can't control people's reactions. My job is to work with my writing and make it the best I can. By the time the novel was finished it was only fifty percent autobiographical anyway. When asked, I couldn't remember if situations had happened or not. They were real in the book, and that's what mattered.

My mother also called. "Natalie, I had no idea you suffered so much. You really lived your life—and all alone with no family around. I cried and cried."

Gee, this fiction was terrific. I was finally getting my mother's attention. I'd written of pain and loneliness in my nonfiction books, but it was story that brought her in, let her forget herself and finally hear what I was saying through a character that was no longer me.

BUT WHO IS LISTENING?

SO, MRS. POST, WHO IS MY AUDIENCE? I know who yours was for thirty or forty years in that heavy brick Howard Elementary School draped by elms in the middle of Long Island. We sat in straight rows and looked up to you a hundred miles away standing in front of the blackboard. I'm speaking to you, so I guess you are my audience right now. Robyn Miller sat behind me and drew perfect horses with long tails and flowing manes in the margins of her notebook. She called all her horses Peggy Sue. Our names were listed on the front board if we received a hundred on our weekly math test. Next to our name was a number—how many weeks we had achieved that exalted prize. I loved to look past the braids, ponytails and crewcuts and see my name ablaze on the board in your perfect penmanship in yellow chalk. I sat in the second-to-last seat in the row all the way over by the big windows you had lined with philodendrons. You were pale and stern in a tight skirt and stout heels. Why am I telling you all this? You were there, you know about our year together. Even if you're deep in a grave right now, you remember, don't you? What is this humming in my brain, this need to talk, this ineffable world I carry inside my physical body that I'm sure communicates out beyond my life and your death, that is held like a dust mote in the air, a swarm of bees, a drifting cloud? Mrs. Post, I'm not angry anymore—or afraid of you. I think you understand this now.

In those days, I wanted my parents to hear me. If only I could speak to them, if only I could express this life I saw, felt, loved and hated. Dear Mom and Dad, dear boyfriend Nicky, dear girlfriends Phyllis and Denise. The circle widened: dear Aunt Priscilla, Uncle Manny, Uncle Sam, Aunt Lil, Aunt Rae, Cousin Nanci, Sister Romi, Cousin June, Vivian, Joanie, Marilyn. Then Cousin Kenny died too young and my push to speak to that tall gangly boy I remembered from Twin Oakes became louder—where did you go? Sometimes I felt when I wrote I could reach beyond beginnings and endings—that death had no dominion.

I never wanted to write to my grandmother and grandfather. They were my audience my whole childhood, not a beat off. I spoke in the moment and they listened. No gap. Maybe it's the gap, the feeling that someone isn't listening, doesn't get it, has half heard us, that compels us to write and explain. That's why we turn around and speak to our past, as if others can hear us now, as if we can finally hear ourselves and catch our fleeting lives. Yes, Natalie, you once were young, you lived in the state of New York, you wore white bucks and never thought of any mountains but the Catskills.

Then my audience—my need—changed. After I met Katagiri Roshi and studied Zen with him intensely in Minnesota for six years, I left, returned to New Mexico, and worked with him long distance for another six years until his death in 1990. I think it was the years we were separated—that gap again—that gave me a new audience. But it wasn't my Zen teacher I wanted to speak to. I wanted to tell everyone what I had learned from him. I needed to translate Zen practice in some way, I didn't want to just speak to insiders. I had to go deeper inside myself. I wrote about writing practice. Could I inspire all those people out there?

A student in a recent workshop read a piece she'd written where there were two stereotypic comments about Asians and African-Americans. I felt Katagiri, my Japanese teacher, standing behind me that day. I had to say something. Being politically correct is not something I'm usually concerned about, but being awake is.

I told the class how good writing comes from dropping below the surface of generalizations to seeing an individual: what color was that man really?

"He could have been mahogany, cocoa, ginger, hazel, bronze?" a student from North Carolina chimed in.

Another helped out—"Oriental is a decoration, or a rug. Say something else you actually see."

I had made my point, but you could feel the tension in the room. I'd lost my audience. What could I do? I had an inspiration. I reached for Wang Wei on the table behind me. I read:

Seeing a Friend About to Return to the South

Ten thousand miles all around, the spring heats into
    summer.
Over three great rivers only a few migrating birds
    soar.
The Han River is broadening into heaven.
A lonely guest takes off for Ying.
In Yun young rice grows beautifully.
In Shu the vegetables are fat.
Leaning on the city gate and gazing,
I see my friend's bright coat, far off, vanishing.

I felt the class melt. I read the poem again. Then:

Moaning About My White Hair

Once I had pink cheeks, now my teeth are black.
Suddenly my white hair is like a boy's pigtail, soft
    and fuzzy.
In one life how many times can the heart break?
If I don't turn to the gate of the void,
How can I purge my heart?

> —both from *Laughing Lost in the Mountains*
> (University Press of New England)

The class asked me to read that one again, too. I knew the mood had shifted. They copied "In one life how many times can the heart break?" at the top of their pages and wrote for ten minutes.

Wang Wei was a Chinese poet and painter who lived in the eighth century. He was a devout Buddhist, but in his simple poems there is no trace of a sutra or belief outside his human life. Yet his profound understanding helped my class so many hundreds of years later. We all fell through our crusted distrust to a softened heart and a recognition of our mutual, suffering, human lives. I wonder if Wang Wei ever imagined us—end-of-the-twentieth-century Americans in sneakers and jeans, holding sleek pens, wearing eyeglasses—as his audience.

In the end, we do not know who will listen to us. It's probably a good idea not to agonize too much about audience—forgive me, Mrs. Post—but simply to write from our deepest, clearest place, to write out of the urge to close the gap and communicate.

When Katagiri died my audience, my vision of why, how, to

whom I was speaking became wobbly. Even though I continued to write—the foundation of my practice—I was in a fog. Where was my true north, my direct connection with who or why I wrote? I found reasons to continue, but I knew I was on shaky ground. I even began a workshop once by asking the students who they wrote for. I thought I could get some new insight. Almost all sixty said they wrote for themselves. I didn't believe them. Maybe they thought that was what they were supposed to say. I told them, "I'm not sure who your audience should be, but I don't think you'll get far just writing for yourself. It can start there but it has to grow bigger."

Finally I let myself float; I'd lost my rudder. I had some wild faith I'd hit ground again. I slowed down. Watched gray clouds fly across the mesa sky, noticed the slow changes of days in February, prayed for snow in our too-dry land. I began to feel New Mexico the way I did when I first moved here twenty-five years ago. My phone stopped ringing so much. I had whole days with nothing on my calendar. I woke before dawn and wrote for hours, then wandered into a café, sipped tea, munched on a brownie, and observed people reading newspapers and leaning over coffee. Roshi would like this life I was leading now. I came back to something simple—I became quiet inside. Who was I looking for? Who could I find? I was writing for everyone and everyone was me.

But still I turn to my readers: I want to take us beyond where we have been. To my students: rest in the structure that holds us up, and keep one foot in each world. Stay close to your own reality and stand also on the bridge that takes you out into something larger— our understanding that we're all finally in this together. Then, who's our audience? Who are we talking to? Open your heart and let it bleed.

Alleviating That Thin
Constant Writer's Anxiety

But how in our busy lives do we get any writing done in the first place? Often, at the moment a student begins to say, "But I have a full-time, demanding job, a family"—I cut her off: "What's the word?"

She makes a little perplexed face. I spell it out: "S-T-R-U-C-T-U-R-E—we've been talking about it all week. *Structure your time*."

Open those date books that Americans are so fond of and schedule in writing time, and be realistic. If you have a busy week, don't beat yourself up for not being able to write every day. As a matter of fact, don't ever say you'll write every day because when you don't—and I promise you, there will be days you won't—you'll hate yourself. Beware of sweeping commitments: they usually have the opposite effect. Rather than writing every day, you'll write no days. Instead, be pragmatic: look at your calendar. If next week you can fit in only a half hour for writing on Tuesday from ten to ten-thirty in the morning, good. Mark it down. Do you have another window of time? For how long? Be specific, jot it down: four to five-thirty Friday. Let's push it further—where will you write? At

the Blue Moon Café? OK, you've made a date, and like any other—
with the dentist, the accountant, the hairdresser—you have to keep
it. You're committed, it's in your appointment book.

Do you see how important it is to be precise? Leave no space for
indecision, set everything in advance. All you have to do is show up,
open your notebook and push the pen.

I hear people say they're going to write. I ask, when? They give
me vague statements. Indefinite plans get dubious results. When
we're concrete about our writing time, it alleviates that thin constant feeling of anxiety that writers have—we're barbecuing hot
dogs, riding a bike, sailing out in the bay, shopping for shoes, even
helping a sick friend, but somewhere nervously out at the periphery of our perception we know we belong somewhere else—at our
desk! Scheduling lets our free time be our free time and not a constant case of playing hooky.

Three years ago I participated in a fall practice period at Green
Gulch Zen Center in northern California. For almost three months
we woke each morning at four-thirty AM, sat in the cold zendo
from five to seven, did clean-up, had a formal breakfast, and then
had a work period from eight-thirty to noon, followed by chanting,
and lunch at twelve-thirty. After lunch I had three hours to write
before late afternoon sitting, chanting, dinner and lecture. Lights
were out at nine o'clock. Talk about structure! I was almost always
tired.

Then came the week I was assigned to the farm. It had been
pouring for days. I stood in the mud in rubber boots and green
slicker all morning, slugging it out with the lettuce. We needed fifty
scarlet heads to sell at the farmer's market the next day, plus thirty
pounds of potatoes, forty bunches of kale and twenty of chard. I
was frightened by so much rain. A constant driving downpour like
this in New Mexico would have dissolved my adobe house.

That afternoon with a satchel of notebooks over my shoulder I headed for the cabin I wrote in. I was crossing the small bridge over a flooding creek, repeating to myself the reasons I should turn back: I've already written four days in a row, I'm exhausted, I might get sick and be in bed for the rest of practice period, I have nothing to write, the bridge might get carried off and I won't be able to get back in time, a nap would be so delicious. I had some convincing arguments. Really, what would missing one time amount to? In the middle of the bridge I almost turned back, when suddenly I heard a small voice: but, Natalie, you *said* you'd write today.

That simple statement washed everything else away. I trudged on down the dirt road lined with dripping eucalyptus trees, up the steep railroad-tie stairs to Martha De Barros's cabin, my writing refuge. I realized in that moment the only thing that gave me confidence—and confidence is a great thing—is that I showed up for writing when I said I would and I'd done it continuously for many years. Several published books, contracts, advances, promotion tours, royalties—none of that bolstered me when I was face-to-face with my resistance. Only the continual act of showing up for writing built my belief in myself.

Now I'm not a person with an iron will. Take chocolate. I have vowed not to eat any more of it at least four times a week for probably twelve years. I don't even think I hear the vow anymore as I storm into the candy store. Every time I say I will never eat chocolate again, I'm really saying, run along darling, go buy a fat dark bar. Why should I trust myself in this area? I've never done what I say.

Let's say, fifteen minutes before your allotted writing time, your five-year-old daughter falls off her bike and has to be rushed to the emergency room for stitches. Grab a notebook as you run out the door, or shift that hour to another slot in the week. You missed it and you have to make it up.

"But it seems selfish to take that time for writing when I have two children who need so much attention," a student argued last January.

A woman from Toronto with six kids jumped in before I had time to say anything: "You're writing for your kids. So they know their mother has another life."

And how do you build that other life? That's right: structure. It's a great discovery both inside and outside the book.

Part Two

READING

SMACK! INTO THE MOMENT

"NATALIE— " Someone raises a hand at a public talk and though I don't claim to be psychic, I can see the question hovering in the air: "What do you need to do in order to become a writer?"

My reply is always the same, "Read, especially in your genre, listen deeply and, of course, write."

Why are so many people surprised by this answer? If we asked a coach, "How do you become a basketball player?" we'd expect him to reply, "Know the game inside out, study players, stay in good shape, practice." But with writing we seem to leave common sense behind. I could say, "Eat two croissants a day, collect spiders and hope your old aunt leaves you money," and people would nod, affirmed in their belief that writing is a profound and mysterious thing.

Literature gives us the great gift of the present moment. As we read we enter the author's mind and follow it like a train on its tracks. If the author derails—gets lost—so do we. But if she is alive, steaming along in her full power, we chug along with her deep into pleasure country. She is taking us far out or far in and

we're there!—no place else. Mind to mind. The writer is concen-
trating—she has been practicing a lot—and we get the benefit.
Mind reflects mind. If we read someone who is awake, it helps to
wake us up. And think of it: while you read you're not spending
money, getting into a fight, creating karma. What better gift can
you give yourself than to arrive in the present moment? I know no
greater delight, and I have lived a rich, expansive life.

But, you ask, isn't the present moment just this: the sun coming
in through the window, me leaning on a wooden desk, my eyes
darting along the page, my legs crossed—not trucking along, my
mind deep in the author's story?

Yes, that also is the present moment, but usually if I'm sitting
there without reading, I am a divided person. Half of me is there,
the other half is out the window, down the block shopping for wild
rice, thinking about supper or how mad I am at a friend. But when
I'm reading and I love what I'm reading, I'm totally connected,
whole. Me and Shakespeare, me and Milton—no time or space
between us. We are one—not two, not split. Then with that one-
ness, full of concentration and presence, I look up and can *really* see
and experience through my whole body the light coming in
through the glass pane and how it plays on the desktop where my
book is, and I can feel my legs crossed underneath.

During Buddha's lifetime, it is said, an extraordinary number of
his disciples became enlightened. Those monks and nuns had a
huge, awake intelligence close by. To have Buddha's insightful mind
as a reflection, I'm sure, immediately increased and intensified people's own awakening. Or, as I once heard a Japanese Zen master say:
"If we're in a red room, we become red; if we're surrounded by
strident people, we cannot keep from becoming angry."

These are confused times. There are few clear leaders; instead
we wander in distress bumping into each other. On the shelves sit

many great books to be read. We can align our minds with those authors and benefit from them.

"But what books?" my students ask. "What do you like? What are you reading?"

I tell them to become friends with a bookstore or library, hang out in it and peruse the shelves. I was in my twenties, living in Ann Arbor, Michigan, and writing my first poems when I learned this grand activity of spending idle hours in a bookstore. It was a Friday in early fall, the elms full of deep color, when I sauntered into Centicore Bookstore on State Street. A bald man named Gary Ireland worked behind the counter, and he nodded as the door swung closed behind me. I'd already been in there six times in the last two weeks—I'd counted.

At first I almost didn't know what to do. So many books—where do you begin? But then I recognized sections: literature, mystery, travel, poetry—ah, that's where I wanted to be. I looked at Frost, Blake, Keats—something familiar, I'd learned about them in college. But this one morning at the end of my week, I felt spry, adventuresome. The night before I'd written a poem about the name Lily and I was sure it was a poem. How could you write a poem and not know it was one? Writing was new to me. Sometimes I was just pushing words around on a page, but this Lily thing glowed; it had a life of its own.

I reached out beyond my English lit training for a lean volume on the bookshelf. It appealed to me in some way, maybe because it was so thin. I thought I could handle it—a relief after those fat, navy, cloth-bound Norton anthologies we used as undergraduates. I sat on the floor, leaned against a post and read a few pages. Then I looked up and watched a man in brown trousers come by in front of me, pull out a book and scan it, then put it back on the shelf. After he left, I stood up and reached for it. *The Branch Will Not Break*

by James Wright. I paged through it—mostly short poems—I liked
that—less than a page each.

The man came by again. He tilted his head to see the book I held.
"Let me show you something." He opened to "A Blessing."

I began to read:

> Just off the highway to Rochester, Minnesota,
> Twilight bounds softly forth on the grass.
> And the eyes of those two Indian ponies
> Darken with kindness.
> They have come gladly out of the willows
> To welcome my friend and me.
> We step over the barbed wire into the pasture
> Where they have been grazing all day, alone.
> They ripple tensely, they can hardly contain their
>   happiness
> That we have come.
> They bow shyly as wet swans. They love each other.
> There is no loneliness like theirs.

I didn't know much about horses, but at twenty-four I'd already
tasted plenty of loneliness.

I continued to read:

> At home once more,
> They begin munching the young tufts of spring in
>   the darkness.
> I would like to hold the slenderer one in my arms,
> For she has walked over to me
> And nuzzled my left hand.
> She is black and white,

Her mane falls wild on her forehead,
And the light breeze moves me to caress her long ear
That is delicate as the skin over a girl's wrist.
Suddenly I realize
That if I stepped out of my body I would break
Into blossom.

With that last line I fell back into the shelves—I was so knocked out. Embarrassed, I looked at the man and he was nodding. We didn't say anything, it was understood: this was great shit. This was language I could comprehend—no references to something in fifteenth-century London. Simple, direct, seemingly mundane—off a Midwestern highway—this poet led me down a road that ended in an explosion.

The man left the store and I kept handling the book. I didn't read another poem right then. I don't think I could have heard it. I ran my hand along the spines of some novels close by. Then I made my big break: I decided to buy the book. I'd rarely bought a book before, except college texts. I turned it over to see the price: two forty-five. Well, I reasoned—and then I had no reason. I just wanted it and went to the cashier. When I hit sunlight on the sidewalk, I felt that I had just been in another world, a place full and close to me. After that day Centicore was mine. I lived in it.

Since then I have sought out bookstores in every town and city I pass through, the way someone else might search for old battle sites, gourmet food or sports bars. I consider the people working in bookstores my friends. If I'm lost, need a good restaurant or a cheap place to stay, I go to the bookstore, confident someone there will direct me. If a town has no bookstore, I feel sad for the place. It doesn't have that concentrated wealth of minds that includes twelfth-century Japan, a painter in Tahiti, traditional North American Indian poetry, memories of war, a touch of Paris and the Mississippi, a lament on love's transiency and instruction on how to cook a good chicken stew. You can live in a small hamlet on the Nebraska plains and if there's a bookstore, it's like the great sun caught in one raisin or in the juicy flesh of a single peach. A bookstore captures worlds— above, behind, below, under, forward, back. From that one spot the townspeople can radiate out beyond any physical limit. A hammer and nails in the hardware store down the block, though fine and useful tools, can't quite do the same job. Even an ice cream parlor—a definite advantage—does not alleviate the sorrow I feel for a town lacking a bookstore.

CLOSE AND CONNECTED

I MAY LOOK TO A PASSERBY as though I'm swinging in a hammock, with my father's undershirts, my mother's housedress, four pillowcases, two matching sheets and seven pairs of white socks snapping on the clothesline nearby. The weeping willow—the one Cousin Venty gave us when we moved from Brooklyn—sways by the patio and my grandfather pushes a new red lawn mower at the edge of our property. But in fact I'm not there. I'm deep on the Bean Farm with Freddie the Pig. Freddie is about to investigate a murder. A female voice calls me in for a hamburger supper. Who could that woman possibly be? This is the sixth Walter R. Brooks book I've read. Do you think I care how this author created these stories? Not a whit. I'm not even aware there is an author. I only know I'm holding a book in my hands. It's all true and real to me. I am in fourth grade. Leave me alone.

But then I'm older—I'm twenty-five, thirty, forty, fifty, and I want to write. I've discovered a pleasure that's almost sweeter than being knocked over the head by a book: absorbing that book with full attention so I understand the author and how she's weaving her story. I've discovered the inner process of how she produced this work.

In the last few years I've assigned books to be read before a student attends one of my weeklong seminars. I have been astonished by how few people—people who supposedly want to write—read books, and if they read them, how little they examine them. It's as though they popped one enjoyable, smooth, round gumdrop after another into their mouths and swallowed, never feeling the texture or flavor on their tongue.

In class we try to get inside the author's mind—who is this person who wrote this book? What didn't this author tell us? How does the book structure help communicate the writer's intent? The more structures we examine the more open and flexible our minds become. We will know there are many ways to build a book. It's not unlike the difference between someone who has studied with only one Japanese Zen teacher and someone who has studied with a Japanese, a Vietnamese and a Chinese teacher. The second person has a chance to see how each country formed Zen and so she might be better able to distinguish the essence of it from the culture in which it grew. At the same time she might realize that a culture and Zen are so intertwined no essence can live without its environment.

This is true of the structure of a book, as well. It cannot live on its own without the organic body of the book and the heart of the author. That is why formulas and rules don't work. Our best way to study is to examine a specific book directly, which is a way to enter the writer's mind. But remember: to study someone else's mind is also to study our own. If we are bored or distracted as we read, it may be an indication that the writer's work is blurry or abstract— he's flying out there with no grounding. What is he talking about, anyway? Remember: mind reflects mind. If he's disoriented, we become disoriented, too. If he's not connected, we disconnect. But if the writer is present, our mind zooms in like a cat about to pounce. We become glued to the words. No place else on earth we want to be.

It's the same when I'm listening to my students read their own work aloud. If I find I'm drifting it's usually an indication that their writing has become disconnected. I tell them, "You know, after she bought those shoes, I went away. Let's look at that part again." Often the writer has shied away because of fear. Things were getting too close and it made them nervous. Or it could have been laziness—"I just didn't feel like going into that." If you dig deeper, you find that laziness is fear masked as inertia.

When I do this kind of listening, I tune my own receptive skills, so that I am better able to reflect back the writer's mind. I find I can trust myself. Nothing is in the way. I learn confidence in my gut response—whether what I'm hearing right in front of me is dead or alive. At this time there is no ego of the writer I have to uphold to make him feel good. No ego of my own where I have to justify and defend a comment I make. Instead there is direct communication: "This is not present—for whatever reason. Make it so."

With practice you can become present in your writing. I remember meeting with my friend Kate Green during the time she was writing her novel *Shattered Moon*. We'd get together on Monday mornings and pick a topic, let's say, pickles, and she'd swoop down on it like a deep-sea diver with no oxygen to spare. Her sentences were immediate and packed with detail. Sitting across from her as she read aloud I could feel their weight. Her continued, determined practice each day on her book made her strong and unswerving. No time for laziness or meandering. Burn through fear, she seemed to be saying.

But what about this fear problem? "I have practiced, I zoom in, I try to burn but I get scared." First recognize that you're afraid and slowly build up your tolerance for fear. You may still feel it, but you become willing to bear it as you write. You keep your hand moving, you stay in there, you move closer and closer to the edge of what scares you.

I believe that this is a primary commitment a writer makes to her writing, an essential commitment she makes to her reader: a willingness to be open to encounter, to experience—and to the suffering this may bring. Isn't this fundamental to any relationship? "Yes, I'll go along with you, even if I'm quaking in my boots or unwilling to face this kind of raw love in my own everyday life." You're saying you'll drop down and touch fear with your pen or in the pages of a book. This commitment shapes and drives everything that follows, and it must be in place even before you brave writing in any form. That *yes* you commit to as reader and writer is the current that hums through all the work.

Of course, you might say yes and then come up against an iceberg. No, you suddenly say definitively. And there you are. What do you do next? I can't answer that for you, but I do know you eventually have to do something—or freeze to death. See if you can chip away at even a little of the mass in front of you—or try standing up on it. Does it support you?

In a weeklong cold winter workshop in Taos I read aloud this passage from Richard Nelson's *The Island Within:*

The first section of road follows the bay's edge, behind a strip of tall, leafless alders. When we're about halfway around, a bald eagle in dark, youthful plumage sails down to a fish carcass on the beach just ahead. He seems careless or unafraid— quite different from the timid, sharp-eyed elders—so I leash Shungnak to the bike, drop my pack, and try to sneak in for a closer look. Using a driftwood pile as a screen, I stalk within fifty feet of the bird, but he spots me peering out between the logs. He flaps out over the water, turns for another look, and then lands forty feet up in a beachside spruce.

There's nothing to lose now, so I walk very slowly toward the eagle, looking away and acting uninterested. He seems content to watch me, or perhaps doesn't care now that he's beyond my reach. Foolish bird: nearly all dead or wounded eagles found in this part of the world have bullets in them. Finally, I stand almost beneath him, gazing up at the eagle as he looks back down at me.

The bird's placid demeanor gives rise to an idea. A gray skeleton of a tree leans beneath his perch, making a ramp I can climb to get closer. His eyes fix on me as I ease to the leaning trunk's base; but he holds fast to the branch. I've never been this close to a wild, free eagle. I think of the ancient hunters, lying hidden in loosely covered pits with bait fastened above, waiting to grab the descending talons. But I seek no blood, no torn sacred feather. Closeness is my talisman, the sharing of eyes, scents twisted together in the same eddy of wind, the soft sound of a wheezing breath, quills ticking in the breeze, feet scuttling on dry bark, and the rush of air beneath a down-swept wing.

I inch slowly . . . slowly up the bare trunk, twist myself around the stubs of broken limbs, until I'm twenty feet from the bird and can't come closer. Nothing is left except to be here—two intense, predatory animals, given to great sudden-ness, for these moments brought within whatever unknow-able circle surrounds us. Perhaps neither of us will ever be so near another of our respective kinds again. I don't need to believe that we communicate anything more than a shared

interest and regard, as we blink across the distances that separate our minds.

When the eagle moves or teeters, I can see his feet clutch
the branch more tightly, and the needled tips of his talons
pierce more deeply through the brittle, flaking bark into the
wood beneath. Two loose, downy feathers hang incongruously
from his breast, out-of-place feathers that quiver in the gentle
current of air. I think how strange it is that I expect an eagle
to look groomed and perfect, like the ones in books.

The bird cranes his head down to watch me, so the
plumage on his neck fluffs out. His head is narrow, pinched,
tightly feathered; his eyes are silver-gold, astringent, and
stare forward along the curved scythe of his beak. Burned
into each eye is a constricted black pupil, like the tightly
strung arrow of a crossbow aimed straight toward me. What
does the eagle see when he looks at me, this bird who can
spot a herring's flash in the water a quarter-mile away? I suppose every stub of whisker on my face, every mole and
freckle, every eyelash, the pink flesh on the edge of my eyelid, the red network of vessels on the white of my eye, the
radiating colors of my iris, his own reflection on my pupil, or
beneath the reflection, his inverted image on my retina. I see
only the eagle's eye, but wonder if he sees down inside mine.
Or inside *me* perhaps.

I take a few more steps, until I stand directly beneath him,
where for the first time he can't see me. This is too much. He
leans forward, opens his wings and leaps out over my head,
still staring down. He strains heavily, like a swimmer stroking
up for air. One of the loose feathers shakes free and floats
down toward the thicket. I've always told Ethan that a falling
eagle's feather, caught before it reaches the ground, might

have special power. I wish I could run and catch this one; but the bird has shared power enough already.

Beautiful, isn't it? This is deeply present writing. But surprisingly, in the workshop I discovered that many students' minds had wandered, even those who said they loved Nelson's writing. Huh? I thought. How come? They defied the mind-to-mind wake-up connection that I've experienced to be almost foolproof. Together we discovered that some of the listeners disconnected not because the writing was not alive—obviously it was—but because they couldn't bear the intimacy. The author comes so close. He holds his gaze on every detail of the eagle—his talons, plumage, neck, beak, black pupil—and the eagle looks back at him: *inside* him, he says. The students felt touched and it scared them.

We need to build our tolerance for intimacy. We think of intimacy, closeness as something good. We can't get enough of it, we tell ourselves. But in truth we fear we'll disappear. Closeness means our annihilation. If we find something we squirm at, we ought to read it over and over until it becomes part of us. Then that work won't destroy us, it will make us larger. When we write, we need simply to become aware when we're moving in on something and to stay there; even if our knees wobble and tears spring from our eyes, we need to keep that hand moving. Do you think you're finished? Keep writing. Thinking can be just another trick to escape. Learn to get close—"every eyelash, the pink flesh on the edge of my eyelid, the red network of vessels . . ." —and to stay in there and hold steady.

MEMOIR OF MADNESS

THROUGH THE WINDOW I watched big flakes of snow fall. Sixty students from around the country and one from England, another from Australia and a third from Switzerland had come to a workshop at the Mabel Dodge Luhan House in New Mexico. This was the morning of the fourth day. They stomped their boots, peeled off their hats and gloves, shook out their coats. Upon registration back in August or September—whenever they signed up—they had been given the titles of three books to read.

I held up *Darkness Visible: A Memoir of Madness* by William Styron. "How many of you liked this book?"

A smattering of hands went up.

"OK, someone who didn't like it, please tell us why."

An Ohio woman in the back, who yesterday had written a funny piece about her small dog Astro, spoke up. "Well, it masked some of the real grueling parts about depression."

A man from Alabama, who had told me at breakfast that seeing the snow on Taos Mountain was worth the whole trip, said, "It didn't go into Styron's own experience enough. I was in a deep funk for three years and I could hardly eat or stand up." Uh-huh, I nodded. More hands were up, but I cut the discussion short.

"Great," I said. "Now we're going to forget all of our opinions. This is a writing class, not a psychology class. A study of depression isn't our aim. Let's make our minds level, like a horizon in Kansas." (A student from that state was in the class and I had teased her several times, saying to the group, "Find out what Kansas knows." In truth, it was I who wanted to know what she knew, living her whole life in one place.) "With that even mind let's penetrate this book. How did Styron do what he did? How did he transmit what he wanted to say? No author can cover everything on a subject— leave that for a manual. Obviously, Styron is not comfortable with personal accounts, or with psychology, therapy, growth movements. He normally writes fiction. He says it right in the book: the only reason he is sharing his experience is that it might help other people."

In truth William Styron is of that Southern White Male Educated class of writers. "You may no longer be interested in that group," I teased. (The class consisted of fifty-six women and four men.) "But the man is good at his craft, he's been at it a long time. Even when he turns his mind to something he's not comfortable with, he's able to do a good job, to communicate clearly. It doesn't matter what we feel, we need to study how he does it. Take advantage of his years of writing, his confidence, his schooling. As a writer you should go to a book thirsty and suck it dry."

I then smiled at everyone to prove I wasn't as cutthroat as I sounded. But the truth is you have to be—not cruel, but hungry, lapping up every drop of those words.

How does Styron begin? I asked my class.

He doesn't start with: I was miserable, depressed, crazy. We might have closed the book right then—ugh, another complainer.

Instead he takes us to Paris—ah, city of cities—on one particular chilly evening, late in October, 1985. All this in the first sentence. We're caught—our minds cling to specificity. Styron signals that he's going to tell us a story, just as if he had begun, "It was a dark and stormy night . . ." Then he takes us back to his first time in that romantic city, to the spring of 1952, when the young writer stayed in a room at the shabby Hotel Washington replete with bedroom bidet and "toilet far down the ill-lit hallway." Now, thirty-five years later, he is about to receive the prestigious Prix Mondial Cino del Duca, given annually to an artist or scientist. How can we resist? This is one of the best and oldest stories: how a poor young fellow rises in the world with nothing but his wits to help him.

We imagine how wonderful it would be to win a literary prize, to be acknowledged and honored for all our years of faithfulness to writing. But the story has turned inside out. Styron is at the top of the world, and he can't enjoy it. In an instant we grasp the real horror of depression. It's not sadness—there are many moments when suffering is exactly what should be happening. Instead there is deadness even when everything outside is telling him to rejoice. He can hardly wait for the ceremony to be over so he can take the first jet home. Then—horror of horrors—he loses the twenty-five-thousand-dollar check he had been given at the luncheon in his honor, a luncheon where he'd had no appetite for the special seafood dish they placed before him, where he couldn't even muster fake laughter and finally lost any ability to speak.

We imagine the French rolling their eyes: what an American loser.

Now we, the readers, are riveted. This is too delicious. We're willing to go on Styron's ride of madness. A writer is a great seducer—how can I get you to listen to me? Did Styron stealthily plan this opening? I don't think so, not consciously. He's an old practitioner. By this time he knows intuitively to choose a high moment to tell a low one. And, of course, he knows the power of story.

But this is nonfiction, someone in the back calls out.

I lean in close as if to tell the real secret of writing. "Don't be so rigid. If you learn a good move in one genre, use it in another. Fiction, nonfiction," I toss my head, "are a breath away from each other. Grab the reader's mind whatever it takes."

We think Styron is now going to go on with the story of his madness, but instead he shifts his focus. There's a break in the page, a new section starts, and he begins to call up a whole pedigree of great artists who also have been tormented by depression. By god, he seems to be saying, he's not doing this alone. As a southern writer he understands the importance of lineage—he is steeped in it. He has Eudora Welty, William Faulkner, Richard Wright, Tennessee Williams, Carson McCullers, Flannery O'Connor, to name just a few, at his back. So in dementia, too, it's natural for him to align himself.

This roll call bolsters Styron, gives him credibility and backing. Why, I look around me, he declares, and everyone's miserable. (For me, Natalie, this is no consolation. It makes me nervous. Why are writers so unhappy?)

Styron recalls Albert Camus, whom he loved, and conjectures on Camus's recurring despair, alluding to his death in a car crash as a semisuicide. He tells about another close friend, the fine writer Romain Gary, and his eventual suicide; of Gary's wife, the actress Jean Seberg, and her overdose of pills—found dead in a parked car off a Paris avenue. The City of Light is woven through these deaths, and Styron realizes that after his own severe affliction, he may never see Paris again.

Now Styron leaves France and casts his net wider. He starts out with Abbie Hoffman. This is a surprise after the other lofty cultural names: isn't Abbie Hoffman too fringe? But it acts—and on this my whole writing class agreed—as a splash of cold water. We were descending too quickly into the dark madness. Abbie, too, committed suicide, but the surprise we feel in encountering him refreshes us, only in another page to plunge us deeper on the descent. Styron invokes Randall Jarrell, that fine poet, then Primo Levi, the remarkable Italian writer and survivor of Auschwitz—how could he have endured Auschwitz and then succumbed to suicide?

More artists: Van Gogh, Virginia Woolf, Ernest Hemingway, Jack London, Sylvia Plath, Anne Sexton.

Most of us who are in love with literature at some point wanted to be these people. Weren't they the ones really living and feeling their lives? How could it have happened to all of them?

Styron has built an elegiac dirge that hums in my blood for the rest of the book.

Only now does Styron approach the word itself: *depression*. Writers do not take things for granted, especially words. They investigate them. In a way, by holding off until this point, he's avoided becoming simply a "diagnosis." He's given us the living reality, not the label. We can't toss it off and put him in a category. We've tasted an artist's suffering; it's buzzing in our veins.

Only after "the word" has been explored and he has declared the lineage behind him, only on page forty of an eighty-four-page book does Styron veer in more closely to his own disease, his hospitalization and his near suicide. Note how before he revealed himself, he wanted to set the stage, to make sure you would read with understanding rather than criticism. This is not simply because he is reticent personally, but because he understands how to lay a solid foundation for his book and then to lead his reader, room by room, into the center of his experience.

Near the end of the class I asked: "Who can tell me what the *physical* structure of the book is?"

The class halted. The physical structure? So far we had been examining the internal structure, but I wanted them to be aware of something so basic that we often fail to notice it altogether.

A long silence ensued. I waited. Then a hand shot up. "The book is in ten sections, marked by roman numerals."

"Yes, what else?" A long pause. "I'm asking something obvious. You don't need to think, just look." Still no raised hands.

Finally, I answered my own question. "Only a small space marks the section breaks. Usually in books each new chapter begins on a fresh page. It's not a major point but it affects us unconsciously as we read." This kind of physical spacing paces our reading and creates blocks of meaning.

In some books this spacing allows for big discontinuities. You can start a new part "ten years later," and the reader can follow. Jump ten years to the next paragraph, however, and the reader would probably feel confused. Yet even this isn't always true. James Salter in his novel *Light Years* sometimes makes a whole shift in scene from one paragraph to the next and the result is a feeling of movement and fluidity rather than discontinuity.

"Wake up to everything about a book," I told the class. "If you do, it will become alive and take flight."

DIDN'T ELVIS AND OPRAH ALSO COME FROM MISSISSIPPI?

I FOUND *FAULKNER'S MISSISSIPPI* on a remainder table at Brodsky Bookshop in Taos on a late fall day. The leaves had already vanished and it was unusually dark outside. In the shop I turned the pages, text by Willie Morris, photos by William Eggleston, and the pictures knocked me out—not because they were beautiful, but because they were so ordinary and familiar. Under a stairwell was a row of attached wooden chairs from an old school assembly, a canister for cigarette ashes at the end of the row, pale yellow walls and spotted linoleum on the floor. Another full-page photo had a broken window, a brick wall, a black-and-white stocking cap left on top of a woodpile and a silhouette of a bare tree across the whole thing—from the intense light contrasted with the shadow I am certain it was late afternoon. In another was an orange-and-white Gulf sign, a flat two-lane highway, one telephone pole and stretched wires, a heavy gray sky and a patch of green grass. The fifty-dollar book was on sale for nineteen. I bought it and took it home.

Faulkner's world was Oxford, Mississippi. He lived there most of his life and out of it he created Yoknapatawpha County, his spiritual microcosm of the South and of the human race. At home I read as evening came earlier and earlier to the mesa and I pored over the photos.

Something about the South haunted me and made me curious. What was going on down there? I saw that many of my southern students were ashamed of their background. I asked one student, "Where are you from?" and she quickly retorted, "Illinois," where she'd lived only the last two years. But as the week crept on and she became more familiar and relaxed, I heard a drawl enter her carefully guarded speech at lunch as we reached for the pitcher to pour water, passed butter and salt and laughed over someone's appetite.

Writing practice asks us to be ourselves. No matter what a person does to cover up and conceal themselves, when we write and lose control, and then read, I can spot a person from Alabama, Florida, South Carolina a mile away even if they make no exact reference to location. Their words are lush like the land they come from, filled with nine aunties, people named Bubba. There is something extravagant and wild about what they have to say—snakes on the roof of a car, swamps, a delta, sweat, the smell of sea, buzz of air conditioner, Coca-Cola—something fertile, with a hidden danger or shame, thick like the humidity, unspoken yet ever-present. Often when a southerner reads, the members of the class look at each other, and you can hear them thinking, gee, I can't write like that. The power and force of the land is heard in the piece. These southerners know the names of what shrubs hang over what creek, what dogwood flowers bloom what color, what kind of soil is under their feet.

I tease the class, "Pay no mind. It's the southern writing gene. The rest of us have to toil away."

But the person who has just read looks up bewildered. I'm just writing what I know, they think. But what they know has a built-in richness and heritage.

"C'mon, Nat," I said to myself that night, the Faulkner book on my lap. "You've always wanted to go to Mississippi. Let's go or someday you'll die without seeing it." I wonder now if I wanted to visit the real South or to enter the country of literature Faulkner had created for me.

I called my Louisiana-born friend Frances and cajoled her to come with me. What was going on down there? I wanted to see the state that supposedly was the poorest in the Union but managed to produce great writer after great writer. Was it in the water?

Mississippi? my friends asked. What for?

Never mind, I said. There's something down there.

We flew into Baton Rouge, rented a car and crossed the state line. Our first stop was Hazelhurst, a tiny town (population 4,221) off interstate 55. Beth Henley, the Pulitzer Prize-winning playwright, was brought up there, and her hometown is the location for her play *Crimes of the Heart*. A newspaper office, a drugstore, a laundromat—normal things—lined the street, but there were also lots of decrepit, barren buildings. The pace of the place seemed to be slow motion. After a half hour of wandering we came face-to-face with a high-shined marble guitar, a memorial to Robert Johnson, so great a blues player it was rumored he'd sold his soul to the devil to make music like that—he was also born in this town! I thought of New Mexico, Michigan, Minnesota, Colorado, where I've lived. I could drive into a small town and it would be a small town—that's it. Here in Mississippi they produced great artists.

We headed on to Jackson, only fifty miles away, home of Eudora Welty, another Pulitzer Prize winner, who lived there all her life in the house built by her family. I remembered that Margaret Walker had taught in Jackson, too. Her novel *Jubilee* had meant a great deal to me. I thought back to being a teacher in Minnesota for ninth graders who read at a third-grade reading level. I told Frances about *Jubilee* as she steered north along the highway.

"It was the end of the school year. The kids' ability had definitely improved, but I knew when school was out they weren't going to bound over to their neighborhood library, charge through the doors and while away dripping summer afternoons in the splendor of a book. Over the weekend I'd begun to read *Jubilee,* a black rendition of *Gone with the Wind*. Absorbed in it the moment I picked it up, I brought the book with me to school Monday morning, hoping to sneak in a few pages during lunch. When my seven students sauntered in at fifth period I didn't notice them.

" 'Hey, Miz Goldberg, what we doin'?'

"I looked up with glazed eyes. 'I know what I'm doing. This is a reading class—read!' and I stuck my head back in the book."

Frances laughed. "No, you didn't."

"I swear, I did."

"Philip, Tyrone, Sadie, Eliot looked at each other. 'Hey, ain't you suppose' to teach us?'

"I pulled myself once again out of the book. 'It's the end of the year. I can't put this down. Please—' I beseeched them and then plunged back in. One by one they ambled over to my desk. LaVerne tugged at my sleeve. They had me surrounded. 'That good? Better than us kids?'

" 'I've been trying to tell you all year—reading is the hottest thing going.'

"Philip nodded toward the book. 'What's it about? Read to us.' He leaned over and sounded out, 'Joo Be lee.'

" 'Well, OK.' I was disgruntled. I didn't want to give up my solitary pleasure. 'Just for a while.'

" 'You gotta, you're the teacher,' Pam reminded me. 'Gee, it's thick.' She reached out to touch the spine.

" 'I suppose so,' I sighed dramatically. I had them in a way I never had before. 'But listen, if I read, you have to promise to listen.' They all nodded assurance and huddled close that late-spring afternoon with the Northern trees finally coming alive out the old windows. I read them how Randall Ware was trying to buy Vyry's freedom so he could marry her and how Vyry picked healing herbs that the white men thought were weeds.

" 'Read another?' Tyrone asked as soon as I had finished this short chapter.

"I looked at the clock above the door. 'We don't have time. Let me tell you about the author.' I pointed to her photo on the back cover. 'Vyry is the author's great-grandmother. It's her story she's telling as part of getting her Ph.D. Her final test to become a doctor of English was on May 20th, exactly one hundred years to the day after her great-grandmother was set free from slavery.'

" 'No way!'

"Yes, I nodded. The bell was about to ring. 'Will you read to us tomorrow?'

" 'Maybe,' I said nonchalantly. 'Of course, I'll be tired. I'm gonna read till late tonight. You might have to read to me.' "

And here we were driving through the streets of Jackson, where the author of that book had lived. I wondered about my reading students—they'd be in their twenties now. What happened to all of them? Did any of them remember their old teacher? Anita had such a round sweet face that broke open when she smiled. And Philip? Maybe, he—there was a chance—might be reading a book, a magazine, even as I thought of him.

We were tired when we reached Jackson, and we stopped only to eat barbecued shrimp and to visit the Lemuria bookstore, where we lingered for a long time. Then we drove on to Oxford; I was eager to get there. On the outskirts, we passed John Grisham's yellow mansion. The people back at Lemuria had told us to watch for it. They said he contributed a lot of money to support literature in Mississippi. Grisham had made it big in a different way than Faulkner had. Grisham was instantly popular, and his work was widely read. Faulkner had been made fun of; in his hometown he was called Count No-Count. The American literary establishment was shocked when they heard he'd won the Nobel Prize for literature in 1949. Evidently, he wasn't sure what to make of it himself—upon hearing the news he shut himself into his house and proceeded to become blazing drunk.

I'd never read a John Grisham book, but I felt a certain fondness for him. In my chiropractor's waiting room, I'd read an interview with him in *People* magazine. Before he wrote his first book, he said, he and a lawyer pal would often sneak away from their office for an afternoon, drive to Jackson, drink coffee and talk about books they loved and their dreams of writing. He said now that he's written these successful novels, he hopes at some point to take a break and write something serious, in deference to Faulkner, the great shadow who hovers over his hometown. I keep waiting for him to do it. Even if he fails, it's the effort that matters. Also I feel a little bad for him. There's a whole publishing machine behind him now, dependent on him. It's never easy to pump out one book after the other.

Now here I was one early-April morning in a blue rented car sitting next to my good friend and rolling into Oxford, passing flowering pink-and-white dogwoods and a few early-opening azaleas. We parked in the town square and found Square Books planted on one of the corners. It seemed like the right place to buy a Walker Percy book, one by Willie Morris and an odd photography book I knew I could get nowhere else, *Deaf Maggie Lee Sayre: Photographs of a River Life,* put out by the University Press of Mississippi. Then we took a long stroll along a wooded path near the town's center to Rowanoak, Faulkner's home for thirty-two years. It was just before lunch hour and the house in a grove of oaks and cedars was blissfully empty.

For a long time I have wanted someone to help me read Faulkner. I've tried him on my own, but I know there are layers I am missing. Often I finger his books, waiting with great anticipation. A man I met at a Zen practice period two years ago said he kept persevering with *Absalom, Absalom!* until one day, "My mind just clicked in with Faulkner's. Suddenly I thought in the rhythms he did and I was no longer in the way. From then on the reading went easily—and it was magnificent." I want to experience that magnitude with Faulkner and I am forever hopeful.

As we toured the house, I was filled with loneliness. I could feel Faulkner's isolation. His writing had taken him to clear truths that were unacceptable in the South that he loved and the fresh form he found to express them was not easily accessible or understood. The creaking of the wood floors, the long staircase up to the bedrooms, even his small writing studio downstairs felt ghostly, haunted by the inner miles, the distance he had to walk to write those books.

The director of Rowanoak told us about Estelle, Faulkner's childhood sweetheart. When she was young her parents claimed Bill was not husband material, so she was forced to marry a proper man, whom she was miserable with. Faulkner finally got to marry her after she was divorced, with two children and strung out on morphine.

While we were talking the phone rang. Frances and I waited politely as the director answered it.

"No!" she said excitedly. When she got off she turned to us. "It was just announced that Richard Ford won the Pulitzer for *Inde-pendence Day*."

"Oh, is he a friend of yours?" I asked naively.

"He's from Mississippi!"

I leaned against a wall. Another one? I can't take it.

After the tour I left that great white house in a fog. I didn't feel much closer to the secret of the South.

We went to Abbeville, five miles outside of town, for lunch. In the back of Ruth and Jimmie's was a good place for southern cooking, the director of Rowanoak had told us. The front was a grocery that sold live bait, licenses, and hunting and fishing supplies.

The menu looked foreign to me, so Frances ordered for both of us. They served us spoon bread, mustard greens in bacon grease, okra, cheese grits, black-eyed peas, chicken-fried steak, and cole slaw on a beige plastic plate. There was a dish of fig ice cream for dessert. Frances dove in and relished the meal. I picked at my food and bought a bag of M&M's with peanuts—something familiar—on our way out.

We crossed through tall dry weeds over to the railroad tracks, where we walked, gravel crunching beneath our feet, trying to make sense of what we'd been seeing. The South was in Frances's bones; she was close to it, but she had as much trouble as I did knowing what her home was all about.

"I can never move back, but when you're southern you also never leave."

We were almost mute, our loquacious friendship at a halt. It was all here—but what? Faulkner had plunged right into the gaping hole between whites and blacks; he dove into a past that was still present. I looked up at the pale blue sky and remembered that sky from photos in my book back home.

Richard Wright was also from Mississippi, from Natchez in the southwest part of the state. I read his *Native Son* when I was a teenager in 1962 and even then I could feel its intensity, how, many times, I wanted to put it down. It was unbearable for this isolated suburban fifteen-year-old, who had no one to talk to about what she read.

What did I want from the South, anyway? What burned in my own life and pushed me here? Sure, there was my affection for my southern students, my close friendship with Frances, my love of southern literature. But, come on, Nat, dig deeper. You're not from here—what is it? What are you trying to unscramble? Why do you feel in such a daze while you travel in this state?

I took a deep breath and let it out: I'm a Jew. A holocaust had taken place here—a long, drawn-out one. It lasted for more than two centuries, making a whole people feel like blunt animals. They weren't allowed to learn to read, they weren't allowed to marry— to dream, to wish. And there was no end to it. Whole generations were born and died slaves. Yes, this was the truth, why I came here. I felt nauseated. It happened on this land—and this was part of my country. And at the same time this land produced extraordinary writers, blacks and whites. And the land holds the truth, has seen it all. So if a person feels connected to place—as all southerners seem to, whether they stay or leave—this land is carried in their blood. They can't forget it. It either tortures and twists them or they open to its certitude.

My heart was beating fast. We'd come to a crossing and Frances suggested we head back to the car. I nodded. There wasn't much conversation in me, but my mind kept going.

If people are sensitive they recognize a great split between what they were taught in school about the grand South and how the place was actually built. They can feel great human suffering in the fields and in the earth. This urges a person to speak, to utter the raw reality of a place. It's almost as if by being from the South, if a writer is willing to contact its pain, the land gives the writer a voice, hands it to her. "Speak," it says, "uncover what's real, reclaim the real story." Even if a southern writer never writes about slavery, it is a backdrop of knowledge, of injustice, a wound one carries. And the South, unlike the rest of the country, knows defeat. It makes a people vulnerable, fearful underneath, as though the foundation of what they've built rests on moving sand. All this is fertile territory for a writer.

The next day as we drove toward Vicksburg I picked up *North Toward Home,* Willie Morris's memoir of his childhood in Yazoo City—I loved that name—and read the first page aloud:

On a quiet day after a spring rain this stretch of earth seems prehistoric—damp, cool, inaccessible, the moss hanging from the giant old trees—and if you ignore the occasional diesel, churning up one of these hills on its way to Greenwood or Clarksdale or Memphis, you may feel you are in one of those sudden magic places of America, known mainly to the local people and merely taken for granted, never written about, not even on any of the tourist maps. To my knowledge this area of abrupt hills and deep descents does not have a name, but if you drive up and down them once on a fine day and never see them again, you will find them hard to forget.

I closed the book and looked out the window at that rich, fertile Mississippi land.

You Can't Do It Alone

THERE ARE MOMENTS IN TEACHING when you can feel you have the attention of every student—no one's mind is wandering out the window, no one's stomach is calling them to lunch. Every cell in their body is attentive to you, the teacher. Words roll out of your mouth and each one lodges in your students' hearts. Even the air feels thicker. The class has moved into eternity. What sweetness!

This happened to me when I told that January class in Taos about something else I discovered about the South. I was at Malaprops bookstore in Asheville, North Carolina, when a seemingly ordinary volume—a book of southern writers' interviews—leaped out at me. I picked it up, leaned near the window and flipped through it.

As my finger arbitrarily ran down several pages I noticed the repeated mention of Louis Rubin and William Blackburn. One taught at the University of North Carolina, the other at Duke. The writers interviewed had either studied with one of these two directly or had studied with someone who had; for instance, Anne Tyler studied with Reynolds Price, who studied with Blackburn.

In his interview Styron talked of Blackburn's gift as a mentor:

He worshiped literature. He saw it as a sustaining force in life. He thought the world of young people who wanted to be writers—feeling, I suppose, they could carry on the continuity of literary tradition. . . .

He was extremely well-informed and certainly well-supplied as a teacher and had an enormous ability, emotional and intellectual, to transfer what he felt about great writing. And he just had this magnetic way of making you feel the grandeur of these texts, whether they were poetry or prose. . . .

We revered him because he made us see things we hadn't seen before. He was an illuminator.

Aha, I thought when I read this, here is another clue to those southerners: there's a secret mentorship going on.

Styron also mentioned a Yale University study, "The Seasons of a Man's Life," that he had participated in during the 1950s. The group being studied included tradesmen, academics and creative people, and the researchers discovered that no matter what endeavor the men were involved in—whether they were plumbers, scientists or artists—each one had had a mentor. In order to progress with some self-assurance, they all needed someone who could guide them, and it couldn't be a parent.

Since the whole class was listening intently, I continued. I recalled an article from *The New York Times* my friend Eddie had sent me years ago. I'd never forgotten it. It was accompanied by a photo of an obviously poor man—worn shoes, torn pockets—attempting to sell gum and candy bars to a group of teenage boys playing basketball on an outdoor city court. The article told of a great nineteen-year-old ball player who played in the summer leagues in

Manhattan. Many professionals also participated in these leagues as a way to keep up their practice. Even Julius Erving played in the games, but no one was like this nineteen-year-old kid. He was a natural, he was fantastic! He could even outdo Dr. J., people remembered. They didn't know where he came from, where he learned his moves. The NBA got wind of him and offered him a generous (for the time) fifty-thousand-dollar contract, which, of course, they thought this ghetto kid would be delighted with. They were floored when he rejected it. Unbeknownst to anyone, he was a dope dealer, and that amount of money was small change to him. Two months after his refusal he was picked up by the police and went to jail. The man in the photo was this basketball player in his forties trying to pick up some spare change.

I told the class I was stunned reading it and called my friend Eddie. "What do you think it means?"

"Maybe we can't do it alone. We can get just so far on our own, but then we have to join."

Someone needed to step in, to guide him, to support his talent: "Hey, asshole, get out of the streets! Drop that dope. Take the NBA up on that offer."

My class was silent after this. It was lunchtime, but no one stirred. I've noticed a great longing for mentorship in the students who come to study with me. There's a lack of guidance in our country and a great feeling of being lost at the bottom of our psyches.

Let them take all this in, I thought. I felt no need to say anything else. We just continued to be quiet.

Finally, the group began to break up and a student besieged me, "I'm upset. What if you've never had a mentor—does that mean I'll never be good?"

A copy of Carson McCullers's *Ballad of the Sad Café* was on the table in front of me. I held it up. "These are your mentors. Authors can take you through your whole writing life. Enter their minds. Don't let any obstacle keep you away."

His face lit up. "I love Robinson Jeffers."

"There you go," I said.

Months later in a Mill Valley library I picked up Styron's novel *Set This House on Fire,* written in 1959. I turned to the dedication page:

With love and gratitude to
My Wife Rose
My Father
and
William Blackburn
this book is dedicated

I choked back tears. His college professor was included with his wife and father—that's how essential this teacher was.

Moving Out Beyond Yourself

I NEVER JUST PLUNGE into reading a book. I look around the corners and see what I can glean from the biographical notes, the dedication, the copyright, the acknowledgments—anything to set the stage.

When I did this with *Ceremony,* by Leslie Marmon Silko, another book I treasure, I noticed in the biographical note that she was born the same year I was, 1948. The copyright is 1977. This means that at age twenty-seven, twenty-eight she was working on it. She thanks "John and Mei-Mei." I'm not sure who John is, maybe Mei-Mei's husband, but I'm certain it's Mei-Mei Berssenbrugge, a fine poet who lived in Santa Fe. Silko also thanks a 1974 writing fellowship—even at twenty-six she was going at it! How did she do this kind of far-reaching work so young? She was a Laguna Pueblo Indian, born in Albuquerque. At the time of publication, the note says, she was living at the pueblo with her husband and two children.

Now that I have a little connection with the author, I open to the first page. This is always a flustered moment for me. I usually have to re-read the first paragraph several times before my eyes take deep focus and the words settle into my brain. I am about to begin a new relationship—wouldn't you be a bit nervous, too?

When I first began *Ceremony* I had trouble. It began with what seemed like a poem: the first word was strange to me, "Ts'its'-tsi'nako," then Thought-Woman—who was that?—and it ended with "I'm telling you the story/she is thinking." The next page was still in poem shape, and it said that within stories is the healing and no evil can stand up to it. The third page was blank except for a few lines at the bottom:

What She said:

The only cure
I know
is a good ceremony,
that's what she said.

I turned the page. At the top, the single word, "Sunrise." Yes, with a period, as though that were complete.

Finally, on the fifth page at the very bottom is what I know of a book: words forming sentences. The beginning of a paragraph that's finished on the next page, followed by more paragraphs—a novel!—my narrow idea of it anyway. It begins: "Tayo didn't sleep well that night." And then it goes on for several pages about how everything is mixed up in him and in his dreams. He has just returned from battle with the Japanese. Wait a minute! Someone my age is writing about World War II, not Vietnam? And a man's the protagonist—how did she know how to enter his psyche?

Then on pages 12 and 13 there is another poem about Iktoa'ak'o'ya—Reed Woman.

My mind couldn't grasp this. I was used to novels formed by
white culture and the way they saw the world. I was comfortable
with that: the story was set up, you entered and were carried along.
This was stretching my brain—I was afraid it would snap. I put
down the book. I thought: another time. But I had just moved back
to New Mexico and already the land, its open emptiness, was
changing the cells of my body. My eye had caught Silko's blind
mule, on page 10:

> It stayed close to the windmill at the ranch, grazing on the yel-
> low rice grass that grew in the blow sand. It walked a skinny
> trail, winding in blind circles from the grass to the water
> trough, where it dipped its mouth four or five times a day to
> make sure the water was still there.

I knew that animal! Ah, so there was something familiar here.
Then I suspected I would return to this book. I saw that reading
Silko might stretch me but I wouldn't break. The book did echo
something I knew and this gave me an entry point, even if Silko's
structure challenged my expectations. But I wasn't quite ready yet,
I'd been living in fertile, wet Minnesota for six years.

When I picked up *Ceremony* again three months later, I was ready
for it. I think I had been unconsciously preparing myself. Does this
mean, if you don't live in New Mexico, you can't read it? No. The
book gives you New Mexico—not only in what it says but in its
structure. We enter the mind of Silko, who has lived here all her
life, so it's actually better than a trip to Taos. When we travel we're
worried about the hotel, the right clothing for the weather, altitude
sickness, drinking enough water for an arid climate, the bus schedule, our flight. We have fresh in us the children's baby-sitter, their
lunch money, the snowstorm in Boston when we left. We are con-

cerned about the right tee-shirt, the right piñon incense, the right turquoise necklace to bring home as souvenirs. But here with this book we have Silko. She's been through it all: the thirst, the wind, the hail, the true poverty and redemption of the land. In her it has been digested: she can take us on a much deeper journey. And isn't that what we all truly long for on vacation? To refresh our mind, to really go somewhere new, to take our life down a new and undiscovered path.

I said I unconsciously prepared myself for *Ceremony* after putting it down the first time, but how did I prepare myself? I settled into the knowledge that I was about to go on a journey when I read the book, a powerful one, and I was going to come much closer—face-to-face—with the place where I already lived, New Mexico. And to experience this kind of intimacy I had to be open, willing to step out of the limits of myself and sink into a story different from mine. I had to be willing to travel the author's path, winding in a way I was not used to.

If you've ever gone to Laguna Pueblo, west of Albuquerque, you've looked out at vast sky and huge undeveloped space. It makes sense that the structure of Silko's book would be different from that of an author who lived in Manhattan all her life. Something different formed the cells of her mind, not to mention that she lived in a Native American culture based on the connection to this land. I was entering new territory and I had to breathe someone else's breath.

There are no numbered chapter breaks in *Ceremony*. The story is one continuous whole—past and present, chant, incantation, invocation, even good and evil. I once paged through a first edition and found a black-and-white picture of the night sky, the way it looked to the main character when he looked up at the vast stars. As I accepted Silko's language and structure my mind grew larger, like that illustration.

I read, "The red clay flats had dried into brittle curls where the standing water had been baked out by the sun." I had often taken delight in crunching my shoes on curled dried red mud, especially out near the road along the Chama River. Here Silko explained how it formed. I'd never thought to ask, and I'm sure no one I knew could have told me, but now I was awake to it: "Oh, standing water, baked out."

I had been shy about writing sex scenes in my novel. I'd sit in the Harwood Library in Taos and write, "He touched her breast," and I'd blush and giggle. After I'd given up for several weeks even attempting a scene (I couldn't bear my squeamishness), one evening I read *Ceremony* for the second time and came upon this:

> He was afraid of being lost, so he repeated trail marks to him-
> self: this is my mouth tasting the salt of her brown breasts, this
> is my voice calling out to her. He eased himself deeper within
> her and felt the warmth close around him like river sand,
> softly giving way under foot, then closing firmly around the
> ankle in cloudy warm water.

Hey, I thought, I know exactly how that feels—recently I'd come back from a raft trip on the Chama.

Then later in the same paragraph: "When it [he] came, it was the edge of a steep riverbank crumbling under the downpour until suddenly it all broke loose and collapsed into itself."

I sat up in bed. Silko used the land to describe sex! She used what she knew intimately to write about intimacy! My mind began to race. What did I know? I made a list: chocolate, New York, books. I chuckled, "He opened her like a good book and felt the page of her skin." Yuck! But at least I was having fun. I'd let sex be ordinary, connected to my life, knowledge and experience. Then I drifted off to sleep, but not before Silko's lesson had registered.

About a week later I sat down at my usual table at the Harwood with a clear intention to write about something else when suddenly I was in the middle of a hot, slow sex scene. It slid out of me. Nell, my character, remembered sex with her boyfriend as she ate a pizza. As I wrote, I was quiet, breathing evenly, almost like pedaling in the street for the first time alone, aware that your big brother has let go of your bike seat. You keep pumping along but don't dare turn around to check—it would shatter the momentum.

I've returned to *Ceremony* over and over, not only to set my head straight about the source of sexual writing, but also when I've felt broken or splintered. I let the ritual of the book make me feel whole again. I'm never ashamed to read a book twice or as many times as I want. We never expect to drink a glass of water just once in our lives. A book can be that essential, too.

You Could Get Lost

A YEAR AGO THERE WAS AN ARTICLE in *The New York Times* that stated: "Reading is the highest activity of the mind." Intuitively I knew it to be true. When we read we not only take on the author's mind and its structure, but we are also actively using our eyes, deciphering words and connecting these words to our imagination, visualizing the scene as we read. Though from the outside we seem to be sitting still, a book opened in front of us, all our mental machinery is roaring away. Our brains are becoming fully alive. Even radio, which isn't visual like movies and TV, doesn't work us as hard because radio gives us the language whole. We don't have to work for it, ponder over consonants, breathe with vowels, stumble through syllables.

"But what about all those books on tape?" someone in my class asks. "I don't have time to read all those books."

My eyes narrow. I lean in to that unsuspecting student, who asked his innocent question. "Do you want to hear a story?"

Then I catapult the class to a time three years ago when I drove by myself from New Mexico to northern California. I reached

Flagstaff a little desperate—there were many more miles to go through Arizona, the state that always made me nervous. Tremendous semis barreled past my old Honda Civic in beautiful, stark country, but I could feel the soul of the place had been sanitized by white America. I'd never listened to a book cassette before, but there on the rack at a corner store was *The Crossing* by Cormac McCarthy. I'd read his previous book, *All the Pretty Horses,* two years earlier. I was astounded by the first fifty pages—the ones everyone else said you had to wade through to get to the good part. I felt the other way around. The rest of the book was a shoot-'em-up cowboy romance, but those first fifty pages kept me faithful to McCarthy. I wanted more of that. I bought the tape and thought I'd have an American experience, listening on my car stereo to a novel about this country's Southwest as I drove through it.

Brad Pitt was reading, and he was good. From the moment the story began with young Billy going out on a cold night to see the wolves, I was caught. I sunk down in the land of the book and my mind never left. I gave the driving over to some Japanese automobile god, because for not one instant was I aware that I was in the car or that my hands were on the steering wheel. I had just filled up with gas so I had a long uninterrupted ride ahead. I only had to eject the first tape and pop in the second. My stereo automatically changed from side one to two, three to four.

My heart was with Billy and Boyd as they rode through Silver City, Lordsburg and across the border, deeper into Mexico. I was after their parents' killers. I wasn't one inch removed when they met the young girl on the road, or before that when the wolf was shot. I rode on and on—not in my car, but with them, with that voice on the tape.

I was destroyed when Billy dug up his brother's bones, and I even fell over the wheel sobbing. It's not right, I said, and I admired how he bore up under such suffering. Then just as the stereo reeled off the last line, "He sat there for a long time and after a while the east did gray and after a while the right and godmade sun did rise, once again, for all and without distinction," my car slowed down and I pulled off onto the shoulder. The fuel gauge read empty. What did that matter? I got out, slammed the door behind me and walked into a late October cornfield, the stalks broken and the field bare. I sat out in that autumn field with Billy and watched a salmon sun cast a high gold on all alike as it set. I cracked a stalk between my hands and listened to its sound and the sound of Brad Pitt's voice echo in my head.

Yes, I said. It's why I practiced Zen all these years. Bare, indifferent, hard, aching, real and an acknowledgment that nothing will save us.

I looked around and realized I'd made it to California—I had no idea how I'd done it—and saw not too far off the lights of a FINA station.

So if you're like me, it's probably better not to be driving as you listen—it could be dangerous. But I do have another memory— this time I was *reading* the book—and I experienced the same dynamic forward drive of my mind, the same complete hazardous whiteout of anything else as I did when listening to *The Crossing*.

I was in Costa Rica. Sometimes my greatest delight is to choose the books I will take along on vacation. I anticipate the long hours lost, not in the sun and surf, but in a book. On this trip I had already read a Barbara Kingsolver novel, a Sandra Cisneros book and Ellen Gilchrist's short stories. I was on a roll, ravenous for another book—and I'd used up my supply. Books in English were at a premium in Costa Rica and the ones left in the hotel lobbies seemed to be pure trash. I couldn't imagine where they came from—none of them were familiar. Then in a restaurant waiting room I laid my eyes on a thin volume. This author I'd heard of: Louis L'Amour. Ahh, I'd always been curious about him. Why was he so popular? Well, here was my chance to find out. I asked the maître d' whose it was.

"Take it," he said. "It's an old copy. It's sat there for years." I opened the book and like a force field it sucked me in.

That afternoon we were returning to San José, the capital. As a special treat my friend and I had purchased two tickets on a small plane rather than on a bus and it would fly over very scenic land. The turbo prop only held twelve people. While everyone else was glued to the windows oohing and aahing over the mountainous landscape, I sat in the middle seat glued to the book. I never once looked out the window. When the plane landed, they tugged at my sleeve—ma'am, we're here. I looked around. The plane had already emptied. I went directly to the van—I was the first one there—and continued reading while the driver waited for the rest of the passengers. They seemed to take quite a while to arrive, but I didn't care—I was pleased—it was easier to read on a still vehicle. When I was finally dropped off at my hotel lobby, the porter asked for my luggage.

"What luggage?" I asked, clutching my book. "Oh, my god, I never picked mine up!"

I raced out to the street and beckoned a cab. I needed to get back to the small airport before it closed. But even in the back of the taxi, I was biding my time till I could be with L'Amour again—it was evening and I couldn't see the words in the rear of the cab.

I wonder, even two years later, what was it L'Amour did? Never had I been propelled like that. All those years in Zen. Even the great Bodhidharma, who sat in a cold cave for nine years—I bet he couldn't have arrived at the same one-pointed concentration L'Amour pulled out of me. Centuries of Asian practice couldn't duplicate the attention I manifested with that book about a cowboy. Mind you, I have no recall about the story—or the title. Vaguely I recollect a character named Tom, who came from the East. I never felt close to him. I never thought about the novel afterward. But I remember clearly and with awe the sensation of my mind that day. It was as though I'd hooked it up to a Concorde jet and was shooting across open space.

Sometimes now when I wander around a bookstore I come face-to-face with a whole row of L'Amour's westerns; shock runs through me and I dash the other way. A warning sign, a skull and crossbones, ought to array his book jackets.

I actually have no quarrel with L'Amour. After all, he loved and knew the West, he kept at his craft a long time—and I did retrieve my luggage. But thinking back, that total obliteration I experienced scared me. The wipe-out was pure, complete; I was knocked unconscious, like unadulterated lust. I'm not a prude. I just prefer to be slammed awake—fully alive in the life of the land and characters. I have respect for the experience, the total trance L'Amour put me in. It had to do with raw story. But he hung on that bare skeleton little meat to gnaw on.

SO YOU WANT TO TAKE A TRIP?

WHEN I SEARCHED FOR *A SMALL PLACE* by Jamaica Kincaid in the Mill Valley library—I had it at home in Taos, and had already read it twice—and found it shelved with travel guides, I laughed. I knew anyone planning to go to Antigua would cancel their trip if they read Kincaid's book. Forget it, they'd give up travel for life!

Two months earlier I had assigned Kincaid's book when I met with students in a weeklong workshop in Taos at the Mabel Dodge Luhan House. Mabel had visited Taos in 1917 where she fell in love with a Pueblo Indian, Tony Lujan, married him and built this rambling adobe on the edge of Pueblo land. She is the woman responsible for bringing D. H. Lawrence, Ansel Adams, Georgia O'Keeffe, Willa Cather and Paul Strand to New Mexico. Sixty people from all over the country traveled here for this writing conference. What did *A Small Place,* about a tropical island, have to do with this gathering that met in January? The students were expecting Southwest literature or at least *Sons and Lovers*.

"OK, why do you think I assigned this?" I chuckled. I wasn't quite sure myself. I'd been a great admirer of Kincaid ever since I'd read *At the Bottom of the River* many years before. "How many of you liked it?" I asked.

Almost everyone raised their hand. "What does she do?"

"It's her rhythm," someone called out. "She could have said what she did in three pages, but instead she drives it home."

"Read something aloud. Show us what you mean." Often when we study a book a good portion of the time is spent reading parts aloud. I cannot tell you the tenderness that is evoked when adult students one after the other stand up and read their favorite parts. Everyone becomes attentive. Alas, our society has forgotten the pleasure of being read to aloud. In these readings we get a fresh direct experience of the writer's mind. It's important when we're commenting on writing to stay close to the heat of the writer's words. Our opinions usually reveal more about us than about the work at hand.

One of the workshop participants read a page aloud where every sentence began with "you":

You emerge from customs into the hot, clean air: immediately you feel cleansed, immediately you feel blessed (which is to say special); you feel free. You see a man, a taxi driver; you ask him to take you to your destination; he quotes you a price. You immediately think that the price is in the local currency, for you are a tourist and you are familiar with these things (rates of exchange) and you feel even more free, for things seem so cheap.

Actually the entire first section, untitled, unnumbered, addresses the reader directly, and as we read, we feel a little queasy: Uh-oh, she's making fun of us. She has broken through the conventional distance between the writer and reader. It brings us close, like someone getting right in our face. But she also lets us tourists in on our ignorance and illuminates us: there's no proper sewage disposal in Antigua. Watch out, that beautiful sea you plan to dive into holds the contents of your toilet and if you hurt yourself, the health care will be abominable.

And believe me, we're not so ignorant after we read this book. In the last paragraph of the first section Kincaid cuts open the whole globe-trotting world:

That the native does not like the tourist is not hard to explain. For every native of every place is a potential tourist, and every tourist is a native of somewhere. Every native everywhere lives a life of overwhelming and crushing banality and bore- dom and desperation and depression, and every deed, good and bad, is an attempt to forget this. Every native would like to find a way out, every native would like a rest, every native would like a tour. But some natives—most natives in the world—cannot go anywhere. They are too poor. They are too poor to go anywhere. They are too poor to escape the reality of their lives; and they are too poor to live properly in the place where they live, which is the very place you, the tourist, want to go—so when the natives see you, the tourist, they envy you, they envy your ability to leave your own banality and boredom, they envy your ability to turn their own banal- ity and boredom into a source of pleasure for yourself.

This is a large-minded writer we are reading. She's also no fool. She knows blame does not only lie with the tourist. In the second section of this potent small book Kincaid switches to the third per- son—tells us of the distant English, who ruled and exploited the island. All in simple rhythm with simple words but the message becomes immense: "The English hate each other and they hate England, and the reason they are so miserable now is that they have no place else to go and nobody else to feel better than." But she does not stop at the English.

In the third section she goes on even longer about the corruption of the Antiguan government by its own rulers. She begins by asking herself:

> Is the Antigua I see before me, self-ruled, a worse place than what it was when it was dominated by the bad-minded English and all the bad-minded things they brought with them? How did Antigua get to such a state that I would have to ask myself this? For the answer on every Antiguan's lips to the question "What is going on here now?" is "The government is corrupt. Them are thief, them are big thief." Imagine, then, the bitterness and the shame in me as I tell you this.

Then her own people's corruption is fearlessly documented, all in that same enticing—you can't put the book down—but ferocious, rhythmic language, so we are unaware of being led through all the repetition like a drumbeat driving us faster and faster into a terrible knowledge. For who can ever go to the Caribbean again after reading this? With the power of her language she is injecting whole political truths into the heart of us. This work moves us— here the incantatory quality wakes us up. We are not allowed to fall unconscious.

One of my writing students sent me an article about Kincaid in *The New York Times:*

> "I'm not writing for anyone at all," Ms. Kincaid said. "I'm writing out of desperation. I felt compelled to write to make

sense of it to myself—so I don't end up saying peculiar things like 'I'm black and I'm proud.' I write so I don't end up as a set of slogans and clichés."

That is exactly what writing is supposed to do—take us into the real texture of life—no generalizations. Why did I assign Kincaid's book to my Taos workshop? I guess I hoped people would make a leap from Antigua to my hometown. Yes, the mountains are gorgeous and we have a rich tricultural society. We don't have the same problems as Antigua, but I wanted my students to be more than casual tourists buying tee-shirts and dripping with turquoise. I wanted them to look deeper. Understanding engenders care. I wanted them to care about Taos.

But something else, too. I wanted them to experience that passion and vision are as important to nonfiction as to fiction, that nonfiction can be as much an act of imagination and exploration and discovery as fiction or poetry—and that exciting language is part of its power. When I say the word "nonfiction" in class, people look at me suspiciously. Nonfiction has a bad rap. We think immediately of those cumbersome textbooks we had to lug through the corridors of our high schools; then those expensive maroon hardbacks we had to purchase in college, the ones that bored the pants off us. We leaned over them in our late teens and re-read sentences—what are they trying to say?—tears running from our eyes, heads felled in sleep, ready to hit the page, our vibrant youth being drained from us.

But nonfiction doesn't have to be that way. I wanted Kincaid to illustrate that.

I taught a weeklong writing and meditation retreat for environmental and social activists at Vallecitos Mountain Refuge in New Mexico. I asked them to write about their fathers, a first kiss, a meal they loved. "Use simple, concrete sentences," I urged. Some of the harder-core groaned. "We need to hone our persuasion skills for grants, you know. We need to get better at nonfiction—facts— for political purposes."

"This *is* nonfiction," I said. "You can't be social activists and not know your dad's death. You can't be environmentalists and not be able to recall how moonlight looks in an oak forest."

"Yeah," they almost succumbed, "but what about when we have to write factual articles?"

"Put those facts at the top of the page or in a list by your side and make sure they're included. But don't just use up paper writing dry articles that no one reads. Please, you owe it to the trees. Put yourself in the writing.

"That board meeting about student rights—why do you care about it? Ahh, so your son was suspended because his clothes were weird—begin with that. Earn the right through specific language and personal connections to finally make a statement about justice and human rights. You've laid the groundwork—now the reader can follow you."

Kincaid says she wrote about Antigua "to make sense of it to myself." Good writing always begins with some kind of direct connection to ourselves. Let Jamaica Kincaid break open your idea of what nonfiction can be.

SAVING YOUR LIFE WITH
A STORY

I OFTEN READ this section of *The Things They Carried* by Tim O'Brien aloud to classes:

> The things they carried were largely determined by necessity. Among the necessities or near-necessities were P-38 can openers, pocket knives, heat tabs, wristwatches, dog tags, mosquito repellent, chewing gum, candy, cigarettes, salt tablets, packets of Kool-Aid, lighters, matches, sewing kits, Military Payment Certificates, C rations, and two or three canteens of water. Together, these items weighed between 15 and 20 pounds, depending upon a man's habits or rate of metabolism. Henry Dobbins, who was a big man, carried extra rations; he was especially fond of canned peaches in heavy syrup over pound cake. Dave Jensen, who practiced field hygiene, carried a toothbrush, dental floss, and several hotel-sized bars of soap he'd stolen on R&R in Sydney, Australia. Ted Lavender, who was scared, carried tranquilizers until he was shot in the head outside the village of Than

Khe in mid-April. By necessity, and because it was SOP, they all carried steel helmets that weighed 5 pounds including the liner and camouflage cover. They carried the standard fatigue jackets and trousers. Very few carried underwear. On their feet they carried jungle boots—2.1 pounds—and Dave Jensen carried three pairs of socks and a can of Dr. Scholl's foot powder as a precaution against trench foot. Until he was shot, Ted Lavender carried six or seven ounces of premium dope, which for him was a necessity. Mitchell Sanders, the RTO, carried condoms. Norman Bowker carried a diary. Rat Kiley carried comic books. Kiowa, a devout Baptist, carried an illustrated New Testament that had been presented to him by his father, who taught Sunday school in Oklahoma City, Oklahoma. As a hedge against bad times, however, Kiowa also carried his grandmother's distrust of the white man, his grandfather's old hunting hatchet. Necessity dictated. Because the land was mined and booby-trapped, it was SOP for each man to carry a steel-centered, nylon-covered flak jacket, which weighed 6.7 pounds, but which on hot days seemed much heavier. Because you could die so quickly, each man carried at least one large compress bandage, usually in the helmet band for easy access. Because the nights were cold, and because the monsoons were wet, each carried a green plastic poncho that could be used as a raincoat or groundsheet or makeshift tent. With its quilted liner, the poncho weighed almost two pounds, but it was worth every ounce. In April, for instance, when Ted Lavender was shot, they used his poncho to wrap him up, then to carry him across the paddy, then to lift him into the chopper that took him away.

Then I say to the class, OK, now write for ten minutes, keep the hand moving, tell me what *you* carry.

When the ten minutes are finished, we pause for a moment and then I quickly follow that assignment with: tell me what you *don't* carry. Notice I begin both phrases with *tell me*. I set it up so students are speaking to someone. Hopefully, the students like and trust me and feel they can open up. Even if they don't consciously hear that request it creates a personal connection—they're not out there spinning in space, filling empty notebooks in a vacuum. Someone wants to hear them. They have to write the assignment so it runs clear. Being clear does not mean getting uptight; it means laying down the authentic details.

O'Brien's book is supposedly a novel about Vietnam. Right after the copyright is a bold disclaimer smack in the middle of an other-wise blank page: "This is a work of fiction." When we read the book we don't believe the disclaimer—but then maybe we do believe it—then we don't care—but we do care. Tim O'Brien is messing with our minds. The narrator of the novel lives in the same places the author does, but even more pointedly he names himself. In one sec-tion he tells the story of Tim O'Brien being drafted into the army after he graduates from Macalester College. As I read I knew the book was all true, but he's also saying what is truth? Specific details?—yes, that's one truth. War?—true, too, but who can hold in the mind the true horror of it? So O'Brien walks out into the land of fiction and looks back and tells the story from that perspective. Maybe then he can get a handle on it. Sometimes the more fictional a writer becomes, the closer he actually gets to dead center. Fiction lets us unhinge from facts and unleashes the soul of a thing.

For my friend Eddie, fiction is his god. When he's in trouble, he thinks of certain characters in books he loves and imagines what they would do in his situation. If he and his wife have argued, he might envision Kiowa or Ted Lavender or O'Brien himself, and figure out what their response would be. It brings him out of himself, his small fight and small perspective, and lets him see differently. Eddie loves to tell of a kindergarten teacher he heard speak. At the beginning of the year her class brought their sleeping bags and camped out at the school for the weekend. For the rest of the school year they told and retold stories about that event: remember when Jimmy dropped the graham cracker into the fire? Remember when Sue's front tooth fell out? Again and again the class re-created their lives. And so myth and wonder were born. Was that camping trip fiction or fact?

Isn't that the way life is? Eddie asks me.

When I bought *The Things They Carried,* held it in my hands and looked at it, I was amazed by the structure. There are twenty-two clearly delineated sections, some only a page long, each with a strong and simple title. Each can be read on its own, but together the chapters give an aching picture of the Vietnam war and what happened to eight American soldiers. Getting to know these men as individuals prevents us from generalizing, "Oh, these noble soldiers who died for the cause." Instead we feel the whole terror and pity of war through these particular human beings. We expect a regular narrative, but somehow this fractured structure slices us open. There is no remote, comfortable ground to stand on. Time shifts as we read: first a scene in Vietnam, then back in the States after the war, then before the war. O'Brien is a boy; O'Brien is about to be drafted. With all the effort of putting things together— trying to make a broken sense of it all—and the slippage between Tim the character and Tim the writer, we become aware of the enormous ambiguity of experience. We feel the huge effort it takes to hold our lives together in the face of pain and loss.

I turn again to the last page:

Linda smiled at me.

"Anyhow, it's not so bad," she said. "I mean, when you're dead, you just have to be yourself." She stood up and put on her red stocking cap. "This is stupid. Let's go skate some more."

So I followed her down to the frozen pond. It was late, and nobody else was there, and we held hands and skated almost all night under the yellow lights.

And then it becomes 1990. I'm forty-three years old, and a writer now, still dreaming Linda alive in exactly the same way. She's not the embodied Linda; she's mostly made up, with a new identity and a new name, like the man who never was. Her real name doesn't matter. She was nine years old. I loved her and then she died. And yet right here, in the spell of memory and imagination, I can still see her as if through ice, as if I'm gazing into some other world, a place where there are no brain tumors and no funeral homes, where there are no bodies at all. I can see Kiowa, too, and Ted Lavender and Curt Lemon, and sometimes I can even see Timmy skating with Linda under the yellow floodlights. I'm young and happy. I'll never die. I'm skimming across the surface of my own history, moving fast, riding the melt beneath the blades, doing loops and spins, and when I take a high leap into the dark and come down thirty years later, I realize it is as Tim trying to save Timmy's life with a story.

Tears spring to my eyes. I, too, have attempted many times to keep my childhood safe, warding off death with a story.

MONDAY BLAZES UP
LIKE GASOLINE

YOU KNOW, DON'T YOU, that basically all writers are helplessly addicted to story. All I have to do is whisper in my friend John Thorndike's ear—he could be anxiously waiting on a bench about to play doubles in a tennis tournament—"Let me tell you about the time I went to a lesbian bar in Madrid," and his head cocks, his eyes soften, his body goes limp. He is pure receptivity; everything else drops away.

I have stupidly fallen for the wrong person over and over because he has a great family story or a hot adventure tale. One man told in a Zen retreat of flying a helicopter over a lake in Florida, but the water was so clear he couldn't discriminate sky from water and so he aimed down and the helicopter capsized. He swam out the window faster than the alligators and watched from shore as the copter sank. We'd been discussing the Heart Sutra—everything that is full is also empty—and he was giving an absurd illustration. I cranked my head to the back of the room where he spoke. Zap! that was too fantastic; love flooded the cavity of my heart.

But sometimes in a workshop the students tell a tale so well polished it becomes boring. One good sentence follows another. Beginning, middle, end. Walk up the hill, come down. It gets monotonous. Even a hungry story-monger like me has her limit when the line in the story is always unbroken and linear, and the structure is predictable.

So, what has to be done when even I can't take any more stories from my students? We have to change the grammar, the logic, we have to smash our minds. Sometimes in desperation I read this poem by Pablo Neruda to my dutiful, good writing students:

Walking Around

It so happens I am sick of being a man.
And it happens that I walk into tailorshops and
    movie houses
dried up, waterproof, like a swan made of felt
steering my way in a water of wombs and ashes.

The smell of barbershops makes me break into
    hoarse sobs.
The only thing I want is to lie still like stones or wool.
The only thing I want is to see no more stores, no
    gardens,
no more goods, no spectacles, no elevators.

It so happens I am sick of my feet and my nails
and my hair and my shadow.
It so happens I am sick of being a man.

Still it would be marvelous
to terrify a law clerk with a cut lily,

or kill a nun with a blow on the ear.
It would be great
to go through the streets with a green knife
letting out yells until I died of the cold.

I don't want to go on being a root in the dark,
insecure, stretched out, shivering with sleep,
going on down, into the moist guts of the earth,
taking in and thinking, eating every day.

I don't want so much misery.
I don't want to go on as a root and a tomb,
alone under the ground,
a warehouse with corpses,
half frozen, dying of grief.

That's why Monday, when it sees me coming
with my convict face, blazes up like gasoline,
and it howls on its way like a wounded wheel,
and leaves tracks full of warm blood leading toward
    the night.

And it pushes me into certain corners, into some
    moist houses,
into hospitals where the bones fly out the window,
into shoeshops that smell like vinegar,
and certain streets hideous as cracks in the skin.

There are sulphur-colored birds, and hideous
    intestines
hanging over the doors of houses that I hate,

and there are false teeth forgotten in a coffeepot,
there are mirrors
that ought to have wept from shame and terror,
there are umbrellas everywhere, and venoms, and
    umbilical cords.

I stroll along serenely, with my eyes, my shoes,
my rage, forgetting everything,
I walk by, going through office buildings and
    orthopedic shops,
and courtyards with washing hanging from the line:
underwear, towels and shirts from which slow
dirty tears are falling.

                              translated by Robert Bly

If anyone speaks Spanish I have that person read the poem in Spanish first.

Sucede que me canso de ser hombre.
Sucede que entro en las sastrerías y en los cines
marchito, impenetrable, como un cisne de fieltro
navegando en un agua de origen y ceniza.

El olor de las peluquerías me hace llorar a gritos.
Sólo quiero un descanso de piedras o de lana,
sólo quiero no ver establecimientos ni jardines,
ni mercaderías, ni anteojos, ni ascensores.

Sucede que me canso de mis pies y mis uñas
y mi pelo y mi sombra.
Sucede que me canso de ser hombre.

Sin embargo sería delicioso
asustar a un notario con un lirio cortado
o dar muerte a una monja con un golpe de oreja.
Sería bello
ir por las calles con un cuchillo verde
y dando gritos hasta morir de frío.

No quiero seguir siendo raíz en las tinieblas,
vacilante, extendido, tiritando de sueño,
hacia abajo, en las tapias mojadas de la tierra,
absorbiendo y pensando, comiendo cada día.

No quiero para mí tantas desgracias.
No quiero continuar de raíz y de tumba,
de subterráneo solo, de bodega con muertos,
aterido, muriéndome de pena.

Por eso el día lunes arde como el petróleo
cuando me ve llegar con mi cara de cárcel,
y aúlla en su transcurso como una rueda herida,
y da pasos de sangre caliente hacia la noche.

Y me empuja a ciertos rincones, a ciertas casas
    húmedas,
a hospitales donde los huesos salen por la ventana,
a ciertas zapaterías con olor a vinagre,
a calles espantosas como grietas.

Hay pájaros de color de azufre y horribles intestinos
colgando de las puertas de las casas que odio,
hay dentaduras olvidadas en una cafetera,

hay espejos
que debieran haber llorado de vergüenza y espanto,
hay paraguas en todas partes, y venenos, y ombligos.

Yo paseo con calma, con ojos, con zapatos,
con furia, con olvido,
paso, cruzo oficinas y tiendas de ortopedia,
y patios donde hay ropas colgadas de un alambre:
calzoncillos, toallas y camisas que lloran
lentas lágrimas sucias.

It sounds beautiful in the original, but I also have another purpose. Since most of my students don't speak Spanish, they're not straining to understand what is being said. They can relax and listen to language illogically. This is good. It creates a small wedge of space that interrupts their brain's driving force to make meaning. Meaning is not a bad thing, but if we let go of purpose we might fall through to the bottom of our mind where everything—good and bad—is propelled with energy and original shining insight. Imagine writing from that radiance, coming from back, under, inside out. It will certainly wake up the reader.

What is the meaning of "a swan made of felt," "to terrify a law clerk with a cut lily," "a water of wombs and ashes"?

My students quickly raise their hands and want to explain.

No, no, I tell them. Normal meaning makes no sense here. Just walk with Neruda's huge and agonizing mind, and stumble across Monday, blazing "up like gasoline." Let things fall apart inside you, shake loose paper clips, staples, binders, let hope drop down near the raw red smell of liver. Open to an inner world that accepts incongruity and absurdity.

I met Barbara Schmitz in Allen Ginsberg's class at Naropa

Institute in the summer of 1976. She began writing poetry in that class. I'd read her work and scratch my head. I didn't know what she was talking about and I myself was slow to recognize wildness when I first met it in another writer. Barbara was "out there" and I was the one urging my friend to "write what you know," in the cliché of the typical writing class. I was trying to pull her into the "real world."

"Well, why don't you write about Nebraska—where you come from," I'd suggest. I was in love with that state. I'd visit her there and think, Jewish girl meets cow. In truth, I wanted her to write my fantasy about the Midwest. It seemed to me that the details of the place—rich dark earth, playing basketball in summer under the light of a full moon, the Elkhorn River—were enough. What was she trying to do? It seemed surrealistic, weird. Her poems made no sense and I think her other friends felt as I did. It was hard to encourage her; yet, she doggedly kept going. Year after year she'd send me her work.

I'd call long distance and her first words always were, "Well, what'd you think?"

I'd try to be diplomatic. "Barb, I don't get them. Where are they coming from?" Then I'd brighten, "I'd love to hear about Norfolk, you know, home of Johnny Carson—you have such great stories about Adam and Bob, Eli, your students."

There'd be a short silence.

"Well, Natalie, it's not quite what I want to write about."

Why not! I'd think indignantly. But I didn't mean to discourage her. I felt frustrated that I could not muster anything helpful to say to this deep old close friend. But, sure enough, I shouldn't have worried. In another six months a new batch of poems would come in the mail.

In the last three or four years she'd sent me a published poem here or there. Nebraska had crept in, but not in the way I thought it should.

Then one morning in July with the phone receiver cocked under my chin—a receptionist had put me on hold—I reached for an envelope from Barb. It was a busy summer and I often grabbed quick moments when I could. I thought I would read one of her poems as I waited; it was in a small anthology of eight Nebraska poets.

The title, "Supper"—already I liked it—something I could relate to. I read:

Supper

> I'm making a tuna casserole,
> adding white and green noodles
> to water boiling in a cast iron pan.
> He's fixing the broken boards in
> the fence. Our son's off playing.
> I resist the urge to go to
> the back door, storm glass
> still on, and wave a movie wave
> across the greening grass, across
> the theater, across eternity. All
> the couples "forever and ever. Amen."
> Repeating this scene, wearing these
> costumes complete with opposite sets
> of genitals as if they were
> real, and we existed, he and I,
> in this time, this old house,
> supper almost ready.

Holy mackerel! The ground below my feet turned to water. Just then my stockbroker got on the other end. "Hey, listen to this!" I excitedly read him the poem in my best oratory voice.

"Hmmm," he paused. "Did you want any more environmentally conscious mutual funds?"

"Later." I hung up and dialed Barb's number. "It's terrific," I yelled. "You did it—you did it! I can't talk long but I had to call."

She was taken aback. "Really, you like it." She was pleased. "Just this week I finished my novel."

"Your novel? Write more poems!" I told her, knowing she'd do exactly as she wanted.

I knew from the first three lines—they were so solid, clear, specific—tuna casserole, white, green noodles, cast iron pan. She had created an anchor—my body could feel it—that allowed her to go anywhere. And she did—she launched a rocket all the way to eternity. This was Barb! This was the woman I knew—midwestern, ordinary—and then in a flash huge, expansive, far-seeing. What I told her on the phone was, you finally matched yourself on paper.

That's exactly what writing is: to be able to duplicate our original mind on paper, with all its odd, kinky turns. Writing is about getting close to our genuine self and the authentic way we see. Barbara had a huge mind—it took her a long time on her own arduous path to capture its extent from ground to heaven. But never fear, she was a midwesterner—she stubbornly continued until the paper reflected her true self.

I took this as a great lesson: not to hurry for sense when I write. I might land too quickly and miss out on half my mind. I think of her in that big meandering country of the self and take comfort.

WHAT BRINGS YOU TO
YOUR KNEES?

LAST AUGUST I TAUGHT *Borrowed Time* by Paul Monette, which is an intimate and almost unbearably moving AIDS memoir. Monette was in his forties when he wrote it. His next book, *Becoming a Man,* another memoir, about growing up gay in New England, won the National Book Award. After that he wrote more—*Last Watch of the Night; Sanctuary; West of Yesterday, East of Summer; The Politics of Silence,* to name a few—all wonderful, all gay-related, all speaking to anyone who is a human being, who grew up, suffered, loved deeply.

I knew he'd written movie scripts and at least one novel before *Borrowed Time*. I wondered aloud in class why he'd received no real recognition before.

Phil Willkie, one of my old-time students, said from the back of the room in a deadpan voice, "Why, Nat-a-line, AIDS gave Paul Monette his voice."

That comment went right through me. Before that moment I never consciously thought of voice in writing. I knew formal creative writing classes talked about it and books on writing style stressed it, but I never much considered it. I surmised that if I thought about it, it would create an obstacle. My tactic had always been: don't think, dive in.

But right then in class I realized a person can work hard, even get something published—but then something crosses our lives, brings us to our knees. For Paul Monette being gay was his early life's struggle and when he met and fell in love with Roger, it seemed his gayness was resolved. But when Roger got AIDS—ahh, now what he loved was being destroyed. Rage fueled him, but rage alone is never enough. It was the outrageous love he had for Roger confronted with the political denial of AIDS, the search for a cure pitched against the imminent loss—all this cut across his throat and released his voice.

Right then I asked my students: "What has brought you to your knees?" The question stunned all of us and we wrote wildly.

I flashed on Isak Dinesen. *Out of Africa,* the book that made her famous, was stoked by the financial disaster of her coffee plantation—she needed money—matched by her desperate homesickness for a land and a life now lost to her. Every page of her book rings with that loss and that love. The two together finally carried her voice.

I told the group to wind down. Finishing their last sentence, they looked up. "OK, now go, write what you love with your whole heart, no ambiguousness, no doubt—what you love all the way."

Years ago in a workshop a student introduced herself by saying she was thirty-five years old and had lived in Brooklyn all her life in the same house she was born in. That fascinated me, especially in our mobile society, to meet someone who stayed in one place. I told her that if she knew what she knew, she could probably write a great book. In Zen it is called settling the self on the self. In writing I think it might be called finding our voice, but what jolts us to finally arrive where we are? I didn't want my students to feel that they must be destroyed to find a voice. I didn't think each writer had to wait for total disaster. What is it that can wake us up right now, can make that Brooklyn student acknowledge her life in that house and realize its value? But it is clear that a voice emerges somehow when we're jolted, loosened, connected to ourselves in a way that's bigger than ourselves.

I thought of my own writing career. In my early years I'd written some good poems, even won a fellowship, and had a poetry book published. I wrote about the obvious things: being a Jew, my marriage to a non-Jew, the Holocaust, my grandparents. But I realized with Phil's comment about Monette that it was when Zen crossed my life that I found a voice. It was when Jewish girl met Japanese straight-backed sitting that she really began to sing.

Did Zen bring me to my knees the way cancer might, or AIDS, or the death of a beloved, or even the fact that my husband was sleeping around? No, not the same way, but it did split me open, ignite me. A whole new way of seeing met my big Jewish heart. I probably had to go that far out to come home to myself. Zen actually brought me to my front door, but this time I turned around and noticed. It gave me a way to save my own life. From what did I need salvation? From a dead suburban childhood, a forgotten heritage? The secret is we're all lost—and those of us who come to writing are searching for our jolt home. It's the cross of gain and loss that electrifies our language—gives it force, direction, urgency. If I had consciously looked for a writing voice, I might have missed it.

The Life of Things

HAVE YOU EVER NOTICED how you first heard of a beloved book, and then traced your journey to when you finally picked it up and read it? It's not unlike the way we connect with a friend or lover. Sometimes it's instantaneous—you see someone across the room and know the moment is full of significance; you'll be with him someday. Or you'll bump into someone for eight years, have occasional lunches, then discover you both are mad for tennis and sci-fi novels, and an exciting friendship is born. With a mate we love to recall "how it happened"—how the connection was made. A lover is charged with passion, so we are more aware of the passage into intimacy, but it's no different from the development of friendship or the final bond with a good book.

For me, it's usually a slow meandering into connection. I'm choosy about what I read. I'd heard about Wallace Stegner. He was called a western writer. I lived in the West—what did he have to say? I picked up *Crossing to Safety* many times in bookstores. Penguin had done a good job with the cover, a beautiful photo of golden leaves covering the ground and some still on thick-trunked trees, a stone wall through a field—autumn at its best. And the book had good, clear print inside, made to lure a reader into sinking in. But then I'd turn to the back cover: "A grand, rich, beautifully written novel about a long, not-always-easy friendship between two couples." BORING. I imagined the smug recounting of four upper-class lives. I wasn't interested. I put it back on the shelf. This routine—picking it up, being enticed by the front and repelled by the back—probably went on for five years.

Then in 1993 I was on tour for *Long Quiet Highway* and had a wonderful escort while I was in San Francisco. I was exhausted from flying from city to city. Some people think it sounds exciting—let me kill the myth right now. It's mostly lonely, disconcerting and disorienting. But then suddenly sometimes something wonderful happens: here I was in this animated conversation with my escort as we zipped across the Bay Bridge. We were talking about books we loved. Elissa clicked on her directional signal. "Have you ever read *Crossing to Safety*?" she asked. There was something about the way she asked, juxtaposed to my having been on the road for a week and a half and so happy to be making simple human contact. "You'd better read it," she said.

I took in her recommendation completely. "As soon as I get home, I promise." And I did and have loved the book ever since.

She also adored *Leaving Cheyenne* by Larry McMurtry, a novel he wrote when he was twenty-three, that seemed to have faded into obscurity compared to *Lonesome Dove* and *Terms of Endearment*.

"That book is one of my all-time favorites too!" I said, and I recounted to her how I'd read it for the second time in the Bahamas. My then-husband's mother had just died—his father had died six months earlier, both in their fifties. Out of desperation my husband bought a package deal for both of us to fly down in the wrong season. It rained every day and when it didn't rain there was a thick low layer of clouds—we never saw blue. And there were no tourists—not even a fool went there in rainy season. The food was a fortune; we ate cheese and bread in our hotel room. Then I came down with one of those knockdown flus. I reached for McMurtry and while my husband walked the beaches alone into his own dark night, I was with Gid and Johnny and Molly in Texas. I became increasingly even, sweet and pleasant while my aching husband continued to burn. I recall that week as a lovely hiatus in my life, a spot when in the center of horror I was serene and happy. McMurtry's book did that for me.

Elissa nodded.

I told her about reading Willa Cather's *Song of a Lark* for the first time. I was forty years old, I had just had a painful operation, and I had to be in bed for two weeks. I opened that book and was lost in a young girl's dreams, traveling with Thea Kronberg to Chicago, to Europe, to New York, poor but determined to become an opera singer. It was a late autumn in Santa Fe and the window next to my bed was open. When I look back, I remember nothing of the pain I was in, only that I had all that luxurious time to spend within the pages of an old-fashioned novel where tenacity, loyalty and hard work save the day.

Then I skipped to a novel where none of those values helped one iota. "Have you ever read *A Thousand Acres* by Jane Smiley?"

She nodded.

"Well, then you know how you can't put it down?" And I began to tell her a secret I was ashamed of.

I was at a meditation retreat with the Vietnamese Buddhist master Thich Nhat Hanh. We weren't supposed to read, only to practice mindfulness, but I couldn't let go of Smiley. I snuck off to a café. Here I'd flown across the country, paid all this money, this great teacher was here in the States—and I couldn't get my head out of this novel. I was reading along: they were playing Monopoly in their farmhouse—what's the big deal?—but I was glued and just then a dear friend walked into the café.

"I've been looking for you. Do you have a minute?"

"Sure," I lied and ripped my eyes off the page.

"I called Boston. Shirley died. The funeral's tomorrow. I knew it was going to happen, but now it's really hitting me." Her eyes filled with tears.

I nodded, tapping my fingers on the cover of the book. Nat, think of something consoling to say. "I'm sorry," I said. It's terrible, but I just wanted to return to that Iowa farm.

Elissa dropped me off at my hotel, and lying in bed that night I remembered a conversation with my friend Kate Green. We were driving up to northern Minnesota, past fields of early corn, when she said, "OK, Nat, name a writer you really admire—someone you can use as a model."

Without hesitation, I said, "Colette."

"Well, what about her?" Kate wanted some exploration.

"She had both men and women lovers; she married her true love—a Jew, fifteen years younger—when she was in her sixties. When she was old, visiting a small town, she went to the movies and someone snatched her purse. It made the headlines of the local paper the next day. Three days later she received her bag in the mail intact—not a cent taken out—with a note, 'I didn't know it was you.' Even the petty thieves loved her."

We were stopped at a crossroads, "Nat, her books! What about her books! I meant someone's writing career."

We were both startled. How could we think so differently? I laughed, "Oh, her books—they're good, too. I guess I'm interested in the life around her work." It was the same as my interest in how I came to a book. The energy surrounding the creation, the human life, was as fascinating to me as the work itself.

Kate told me how she admired Anne Tyler. "Nat, I love the subjects she explores in her *books*," the emphasis to tease me. "Forget about the aura around the author." There was no right or wrong about our approaches—one looked at the dead center, the book itself, and the other looked at the journey to the book.

Hyperion, a New York publisher, had sent me the uncorrected proofs of a book called *Seeds from a Birch Tree*. They hoped I'd write a blurb. I stood in my kitchen by the window. Hmm, about haiku. "Write them that I can't do it." I handed it over to my long-time assistant, Jean Leyshon.

Over the years I've found that Jean doesn't throw things out. She cuts up old manuscripts for scrap paper; I once found wandering Jew plants in water jars all over my kitchen. She'd pulled them out of the planter.

"I thought we were getting rid of these?" I asked, pointing.

"We can't just throw them out, I had to think of the most compassionate way to dispense with them," she explained.

"Of course," I said, swallowing my opinion of the plant that had choked my bougainvillea.

Six months later over lunch she casually mentioned, "You know, that book on haiku," she took a gulp of water. "It's the best book on Zen I've read in years."

"What book on haiku?" I stopped my sandwich in midair.

"The one they sent you. My computer table was rickety so I used it as a leg stop. Then last week I had to move the table. I picked up the book and started reading." She shook her head. "Amazing book."

"Where is it? I want to see it."

This is the odd way I came to Clark Strand's book, but Jean was right. The book brought me back to my first taste of sitting Zen, my early love of writing, and the way I picked up my first paintbrush. All at the age of twenty-six when my worlds collided and then shone in a whole new way. I was curious, slow and awake then and understood life to be personal and real.

In the last paragraph of his introduction Clark Strand writes:

> If I had to identify the thread that runs through the book, I would have to say that it is sometimes haiku, sometimes the story of my life, and often both at once. For that is the nature of the spiritual path: it happens to someone, somewhere, in a very particular way. Yet, the episodes are not chronological. Often, in retrospect, it was the things that happened at the beginning that seemed most important later on. And if the reader should notice that many of the episodes concern things (events, people, even parts of myself) that seemed insignificant at the time and only later were realized to be essential parts of the path of haiku, then he or she would not be off the mark. In a world where everything is living, nothing can be thrown away. Where would you throw it *to*?

Bingo! He gives the secret to his structure. Writers! pay attention. Intermixed we learn of Zen, of poetry, of Clark Strand, a person who practices both. Interwoven is who he met, what he thinks, how haiku is formed.

My journey to discovering Clark's book matched the way Clark came to haiku: backward. And my guess is: this is how we come to most things that finally matter, especially books we love.

LOTUS IN MUDDY WATER

I CALLED CLARK STRAND after I read his book and the next time I was in New York we met. It turned out he was southern.

I leaned over the small table where we were sitting—the rain out the large storefront window was thundering down on the street—"Do you love Carson McCullers the way I do?" That is my final test. The person can't skip over to other southern writers, Flannery O'Connor or Tennessee Williams, though they're fine, too. They have to know the goodness of Carson.

He nodded deeply.

"Did you know she's buried in Nyack, New York? Next time I come, let's go find her grave."

We made a vow to do it.

If possible I like to visit an author's grave and see where they've ended up. Where does this life of writing take us?

Seven years ago I flew down to Ecuador to find Moritz Thomsen. I was lucky enough to have met his niece Rashani, and American Airlines had a huge sale on fares to South America. Off we flew to Guayaquil—probably the armpit of the country. No tourist in his right mind would travel there, but, hey, if you've just read *Living Poor,* Thomsen's Peace Corps chronicle, followed by *The Farm on the River of Emeralds,* you'd gladly go to Guayaquil to meet this author.

In his forties Thomsen had spent six years in the Peace Corps in the Ecuadorian jungle; then at the age of fifty-three he returned to the jungle and began a farm on the Esmeraldas River with Ramón Prado, a poor black man twenty years younger.

Now in his early seventies, Rashani told me, he was living in slum housing in the thick center of the city. She had no address for him, but she knew he was dying of emphysema. We went to the local bookstore—the place she had written him over the years—and hoped we could be shown the way to his place. The owner sent a young clerk with us and we walked down the noisy, then more quiet, broken streets. A dead pig was draped over the back of a parked motorcycle, where we turned and walked up a grimy staircase. The boy pointed to a dirty white door.

My friend and I looked at each other. "Here goes," she said and knocked.

After a few moments someone yelled, "Who is it?"

"It's your niece, Rashani." In the long silence we could feel the disbelief, the confusion. "Moritz, didn't you get my letter?"

The door opened a crack, held by a tight chain, and a man peered through—intense, awake eyes, a hooked nose, naked to the waist, wearing dirty jeans. The door shut a moment and then opened wide. "I never got any mail. Come in." He nodded to the clerk. "It's OK now," and the thin youth flew down the stairs.

The room had three chairs, a table by the wall, dirty windows onto the street, two wilting green plants on the ledge, a stereo with lots of albums—I remembered from his books how he adored classical music—and a crammed bookshelf.

"How long has it been?" His eyes fed on his relative as though she were a vision. He was in his early seventies, but he still had a wiry, strong build and his skin was as dark as if he'd just spent a summer in the fields. "Gee, I have nothing to offer you." He opened his fridge. "I mostly boil some hot dogs."

"We're here to help. We'll feed you. Where's a nearby market?"

He'd made a commitment to live in poverty and now there was no turning back. He couldn't go up and down the stairs because his lungs had given out, so he was dependent on a few kids he tipped to bring him medicine and food. His real friends were in Quito, but after fifty years of smoking, the ten-thousand-foot altitude was too much for his chest. He was banished to the coast, to Guayaquil, for the remainder of his life. He'd been in this apartment for two years.

We went to open stalls that lined a street adjacent to his and carried armfuls of radishes, bread, corn, bananas, cheese, milk, eggs, tomatoes into his apartment and made him omelettes and banana smoothies. We could find his place easily now—among the squalor of dark gray, square tenements his was the one where Shostakovich blasted out of the windows.

We found a terrible, cheap—they all seemed terrible and cheap—hotel, two blocks away, and fell into a daily routine of visiting him in late morning, staying through early afternoon, and then returning in early evening.

He loved talking books—Proust, Chekhov, Bellow, Roth—and told us of Page Stegner and Paul Theroux, whom he knew and admired.

At one point I said, "Moritz, you're an underground cult figure in the States. When I told my friend John Thorndike that I was coming to see you, he said it was because of reading your books many years ago that he went down to Chile and started a chicken farm."

Moritz looked at me askance. I realized he'd never come back to the States, never done a reading or a book signing—the normal things an author experiences. He received few fan letters. Without an address there was no way to reach him and he didn't have a phone.

"Moritz," Rashani said quietly, "why don't you come home with us. You'd like New Mexico and I could take care of you. Young writers would love to talk with you. You could be happy."

"Happy?" He stared her down. "You can't expect happiness. If it comes along—consider yourself lucky, but that's not what life's about."

His body wasn't well, but his mind was steel clear. It felt as though he'd heeded Hemingway's dictate: write clear and hard about what hurts. I'm sorry I didn't take the opportunity just then to ask him, then what is life about, Moritz?

He was working on a manuscript called *My Two Wars,* juxtaposing his tumultuous relationship with his father and his stint as a bombardier in the Eighth Division of the United States Air Force. He read us parts while we sat at his table. His father had been domineering and wealthy but only left Moritz a small inheritance, most of which he lost on the jungle farm. The rest he had put in trust for Ramón's two kids.

Rashani and I took a break for a few days and rode a bus to Quito. Ramón's ex-wife, Ester, who had been close to Moritz when they lived on the farm together, had started a restaurant there. Moritz had found the location for her:

At that time I lived in a lively neighborhood where six streets met at one of those crazy little traffic-stopping circular parks. It held a dozen or so cement benches upon which on clear mornings old men—of whom I was now one—sat in the sun and gazed at the Andes rising up like a wall just past the end of Madrid Street, gazing at that particular spot (marked by the aluminum cross of a crashed army plane) where the local geologists were predicting that any day now the sleepily steaming volcano called Pichincha would split open and bury us all in a river of mud, all of us in the city transformed instantly into hot fudge sundaes. Just behind the benches, there was a round pool, dry in the dry season but in winter full of deadly green water in which schools of plastic cups and the scraps of old newspapers swam and bred. One day a FOR SALE sign appeared in one of the shops below an almost new ten-story apartment building. It was an ideal locale for a restaurant, for it was a business center centered around a hundred small shops. It had a view of the park and the mountains and the constant stream of spinning traffic, and it was large enough for ten tables. It was also outrageously expensive.

For over a year, too poor now to eat anyplace else, I lived on Ester's shrimp *ceviche,* her slabs of fried sea perch, in the restaurant I had helped her buy and where I had unlimited credit. For the first six months, as her business grew and prospered, I engaged in what was, aside from a year spent dropping bombs on Germany, some of the most constructive work of my life—waiting on tables and washing dishes. Later, sitting in the park and between waiting for the mountain to explode and contemplating the plastic cups as they copulated in the stagnant water, I could look across the street and watch Ester getting rich. It was one of my few good deeds that ended as so few had—the way it was supposed to, its planned objectives achieved.

This was in the postscript for *The Farm on the River of Emeralds,* written long after the farm was sold and Ramón had a new wife and his and Ester's children were grown. The taxi couldn't find Ester's place with the address we had. I whipped open Moritz's book and Rashani translated into Spanish "below a ten-story apartment," "view of the park and the mountains," circular park, end of Madrid Street, cement benches, round pool. I held my breath—was Moritz's writing true even on this practical level? Sure enough! We managed to find the small café.

I was forty-two years old. My second book had just come out. I'd given it to Moritz—he'd read it and liked it. I was relieved. Moritz didn't mince words and could be very critical. My Zen teacher, Katagiri Roshi, had died eight months before. I was about to begin my third book. I had dedicated myself to the written word. Was it a good choice? Was there something better? I didn't know. Moritz was near death, living alone and in squalor, but I wasn't scared, because his mind was so clear, as though at some point he'd looked down to the bottom of the well and rested in that. I liked to believe it was writing that took him there. The long quiet hours of sitting meditation I knew took Roshi there. I had chosen writing as my primary path rather than being a monk and hoped I hadn't abandoned my way to clarity. Moritz was my bright pearl, my lotus in a pond of muddy water. Writing sustained his diamond life. If I could trust his example, whatever his outside circumstances, I had chosen well.

After three weeks we left Ecuador and I received letters in black ink on white paper with his small uneven script. I'd sent him three early Larry McMurtry books:

Yes, I liked *Goodbye to Cheyenne* [he meant *Leaving Cheyenne*]. Then I started *The Last Picture Show*—which I preferred. I thought the relationship between the aging woman and the kid was pretty terrifying stuff. All love stories end as terror stories if they're good. The truth about love is that the screwing you get isn't worth the screwing you get. All that agony at the end. The madness, the screams, the tears, the jealousy. And, of course, love without all the final death agony is just cold hearted fucking.

(dated 24 May 1991)

Re-reading his letters I'm reminded how caustic Moritz could be. Sharpness is good but there's a danger for writers. So much workout with the notebook and pen, while taking us deep into our own minds, can leave us a little dry, a little removed from human life, so that we observe circumstances from a slight distance. We're making love and thinking how we can write about it. And even if it's one millimeter separation, that can make the difference between heaven and hell. I think that Moritz with his steely clarity sometimes suffered in his own inferno.

On June 24, 1991, Moritz wrote another letter, telling me that though he felt McMurtry wrote about limited subjects, "he has an awful charm and I wish I could figure that out." I want to say the same back to him—Moritz, you have an "awful charm" and one is drawn to you. He threw his life totally into the life of Ecuador and then into his writing—he exposed all aspects of himself fully, as a naive fool, as a hungry dreamer, as a lean man full of desire. His raw honesty drew me to him; yet, his inability to soften, to admit loneliness or his need for care and nourishment haunts me. Where do our lives take us?

He died a few months after this last June letter.

Part Three

REINING IN YOUR
WILD HORSES

CEMETERIES, NIGHTCLUBS AND WORN SHOES

WRITING PRACTICE LETS OUT all your wild horses. Everything you never dared to utter—didn't even know you thought—comes galloping and whinnying across the page. This is good. You become connected with a much larger force field, one where you're not in control. Suddenly your little will is not doing the writing, but instead writing does writing. The trees and skies, cemeteries, night-clubs, barns, old loves and worn shoes step forward and take their true positions.

I advise students to do only writing practice for two years to get in touch with their wild minds—to discover their true longings and fears. It's a strong foundation for writing; something you can rely on and go back to over and over.

Often the students balk—two years? But I'm taking this time to write—I have to prove myself. I have to publish, do meaningful work. I can't just fill notebooks.

Would you expect to play Wimbledon your first week ever on the court? I ask them. Trust me, this practice will make you strong.

And what about those of you who've already written short stories, articles, a novel and then come to a dead end? I say submerse yourself in writing practice for a good six months—nothing else—to get the juices flowing again. You'll learn new footwork, a looser swing.

Then when my students are still grimacing—two years? that's twenty-four months—tell them to think of me. I dumbly filled notebooks for thirteen years! Going nowhere, lost and fascinated with my own mind. Yes, I agree, looking back, maybe ten would have sufficed—I was a bit indulgent. But that was my generation. Now people are more efficient. Give yourself a good two years. Promise me.

From time to time after you fill a notebook, read it over. Underline lines you like—you may use them as topics for future writings. I remember living in the Twin Cities and discovering the line "I came to love my life" written in one of my notebooks. I was actually miserable at the time, but that one line had tremendous energy for me and I did many timed writings taking off from there. What did I mean by it? Why was I so drawn to it? In the middle of distress, was I not noticing that a true jewel was being born, that I'd come "to love my life"?

You might even find a whole poem burning on the page. If so, type it up. But above all take this opportunity to meet your own mind. Hello! So this is what I really care about, think about? Get to know your obsessions. They have the power and energy that may eventually carry you through the arduous task of writing short stories, essays, even a novel. Ask yourself, what monopolizes my mind? Be honest and ride that passion, whatever it is.

I have noticed that students skip this process of reading their notebooks. They want to be active and Write! Write! Write! They've finally contacted paper with pen, sometimes after years of inertia, procrastination, fear. Now they are determined to gallop ahead. Let me finally blaze my trail, they seem to say. I'm afraid if I stop to see what I'm writing, I won't like it. I'll quit.

I understand the panic, but the anxiety actually grows, as though an eerie ghost is chasing us, if we don't finally turn around and behold ourselves. Reading our notebooks is a way to digest and close the gap, so we don't feel like we're always running ahead of an abyss.

I like to take my notebooks to a café, order a large cup of hot chocolate and a croissant, and hunker down into my terrible hand-writing and see what I'm about. Yes, sometimes I'm unbearably boring. I just note it: "Nat, darling, give me a break. Switch to an ice cream sandwich—anything—sooner, quit complaining for so many pages." And sometimes I'm humbled by my earnestness, my fascination with empty small towns and the states of North Dakota and Nebraska. But most important, I'm sitting there for several hours having a relationship with myself. In my busy life, I'm stop-ping, I'm receiving. I see that while I think I'm the active one, always doing, creating, I am also the one being created. I see that writing does writing—that who and how I am is out of my control. This allows me to relax more and accept the writing that comes through me.

I've also found it helpful to do a ten-minute timed writing right after I've finished reading a notebook. I just note what I've read:

I see I'm avoiding my relationship with Tim. I keep saying he's "nice." He's not nice; he's a bastard, but honest. I like that about him. I see that no matter what I write about I come back to Katagiri Roshi. I still don't understand why he died. The writing about him is vague and disjointed and lacks detail, but when I write about my writing process—my real practice—I'm clear and articulate, like suddenly I know who

I am. And I see I like men and women with equal fervor.
Though I hate the word bisexual—it's like bionic man—I prefer omnisexual. I guess there was some point through writing
when I went so deep in my concentration I broke down long-
held beliefs and barriers. I like when I write out beyond
myself, but can my writing also build up some healthy boundaries? Yes, I believe it can. I loved reading about Bob's trying
to answer the Rhinoceros Fan koan when I told it to him during my last visit to Norfolk. I still can't believe he threw lit
firecrackers into my room at 6 AM. What did he think? The
answer to the Zen koan would explode in my face?

These short writings after reading a notebook are often intro-
spective, a place where I absorb my mind. It's here that I can
develop a depth and richness to what I know and I've found this
process layers and deepens what I have to say.

Students in a May class made a list of the following questions that
each person wanting to write should eventually be able to answer:

What's really important to you?
What are the subjects that really pull you?
What are you willing to be witness to—to stay in there and
    carry for a long time?
What are you the most afraid to write about?
What is your darkness?
Whom do you write for?

These questions get at the fruit of spending two years just writing. We find out what's really alive for us, not what we think we
"should" be writing or our self-image of what kind of writer we'd
like to be.

Now after two years of writing practice we've opened our minds, and they're huge fields with pintos and stallions running wild. Before doing this practice we whined—what can I write about? We felt lifeless. Now we have vast landscapes of stormy, sweaty, fertile heated energy. Ahh, very good; we can take the next step. It is time to bridle that stampede, pick up the reins and slowly take control of that power.

But don't expect a smooth ride right away. A wild horse will buck and rear. Hold the reins loosely. Before, you might have begun with "I remember" and let any memory from the whole universe and your life tumble onto the page. Now begin an "I remember" exercise but stay only with memories of 1986 or fifth grade or that lunch in Manhattan with Polly last August—that one specific meal at one specific place with one person. Accustom your wild mind to taking direction.

It's as though for two years we have flooded, let's say, the whole state of Ohio indiscriminately—cities, towns, farms, highways, hills, forests. Now the next step is directing that energy down specific glens, valleys, creeks, ravines. We don't want to reduce the strength of the stream—we simply want to engineer it. Remember those questions. Let your answers motivate you to start channeling your writing.

But let's say you're doing a directed "I remember" writing practice on chicken soup and a single tree you once crouched under in a storm keeps lunging through your mind. You think, stay out, I'm into the broth in the bowl—but it persists. Then give it room, digress—you understand your mind through practice. That tree might eventually plunge you deeper into the soup, that rainstorm in Colorado might have something to say about the streets in Brooklyn, your grandmother's thin-skinned hands that sold yellow capons and the celery leaves she chopped and added to the boiling stock. You direct, but you also give a wide berth. You find your own balance.

For six years I attended Katagiri Roshi's lectures every Wednesday evening and Saturday morning. Each time he'd begin with reading from the *Blue Cliff Record,* a collection of one hundred Zen teachings of Chinese Zen masters compiled in the twelfth century, then he'd take off for an hour in an entirely different direction—Timbuktu, East Hosh Kosh, or at least Tokyo. Surely, I thought, the man is lost. But then just in the last moment or sentence he'd snap back to what he'd begun with. If I wasn't careful, I would get whiplash.

Ahh, so he wasn't confused. He'd been in charge all along, only with a loose rein.

WRITING AS A VISUAL ART

TO PICK UP THE REINS and begin to guide your galloping wild horses, moving from rampant writing to harnessing the expression of your large mind, means also to take on a certain responsibility as a writer. I'm not saying that this is the moment to begin carrying the burden of literature and deciphering the meaning of Western civilization. I'm only saying that the clear water, the vast trough of freedom you have been abundantly gulping down in your two years of practice has now been tainted—ever so slightly—with accountability. (Don't kick and rear when you hear that word.) It's time to claim the force of your own power. It's your mind, after all, that has been enjoying resplendent liberty and self-determination—running free in the fields of your notebooks. Now you have to show your stuff—direct your mind down a path. The reins are in your hands. You want someone else to listen, to see and feel the world as you do. How do you make that happen?

Here is a good exercise: imagine a scene as a photograph—the moment a husband tells his wife he's just been fired from his job—and describe what you see. You cannot say, "She was shocked and

furious." You cannot say, "She was sympathetic." These are not pictures. We are trying to bring the scene vividly alive in the reader's
mind. Instead, focus on the face of the woman in the photo: her
lower lip is curled, ringed hand stretched out toward the man
across the couch, eyes narrowed in slits. What does he look like?
What are they wearing? And the room? Flowered carpet? Black-
and-white linoleum? Fern in the corner? Window open? Ceiling
fan? Probably that photo will not reveal whether it's in Illinois or
Florida—unless there's a palm tree out the window. We cannot
know what the photo does not directly impart. No past or future is
in a picture, only the revelation of the moment. Don't let wild
mind travel off into introspection—what could have happened?—
or imagine how she is feeling or how he is feeling. Stay with what
is given. The reader will glimpse the feelings far more immediately
in the gesture—the curled lip, the outstretched arm—than in any
abstract statement. Here we are developing writing as a visual art,
using our eyes as the primary way into a scene. Begin to rein your
horses in that direction. This does not mean your eyes are the only
entry point, but the visual world is a good grounding for your own
writing and an effective way to reach the reader.

In writing practice we are allowed to express everything about a
situation. If we like, we can go on for three pages about how we
hate the photo, then skip to the boss who once fired us, then to our
aching back, the saltshaker, our true love, the dog we lost. But now
we are writing for a reader, and the new taste of responsibility is in
our mouth. There is another person here. We have to communicate,
get the picture across. How best to get that result? Practice freezing moments or situations as photos. Step through the abstract
names for emotions—shocked, furious—and touch the details.

I peruse the yellow slips stuck to the right margins of my last manuscript, where my editor comments as she line-edits. The most frequent note is some version of *get clear:*

Very dull and fuzzy in expression—*distant*. Can you fix?
Could be more vivid.
We need one really good, precise adjective to get across the quality of the vase.
Location of these thoughts not clear—in the car or Aunt Priscilla's?
No need to categorize or compare—just stay with the experience.
Get a little closer to this—the physicality of it.
Can you be more precise? [this comment on many slips throughout the manuscript]
Sharpen.
This seems diffuse. Vague. Can you tighten?
This doesn't say anything specifically about your father.

I have before me a Walker Evans photo taken in Alabama in 1936. First I'll do writing practice with it:

There's a family sitting in a row in a wood cabin. They look beat and poor and dirty. This picture is depressing. I'd rather think about my own family or my dream last night. When I think of poverty I get sad—how can someone go unfed in this country—there's so much waste. I'm hungry right now. I didn't have a big dinner last night. I feel old today. My shoulders are tight. Maybe it was the Depression that made them so poor. Dirty too—smudged clothes. I remember when I was a hippie and had a woodstove and no running water. My clothes kinda looked like theirs—smudged with smoke, ash and wood coal. I could never keep anything clean. I dreamed last night that an old woman tried to make love to me. I was sort of interested.

This is diffuse, unfocused—we don't learn much about the actual photo. My wild horses are moseying over to other pastures—how I feel, how the photo relates to me.

Now I pick up the reins and direct the horse to stay in front of the picture:

A woman in a checked dress sits on an unmade iron bed with a child—about two—splayed across her lap, sleeping. The woman is leaning forward, shoulders hunched, bare feet crossed at the ankles. A girl, maybe eight, long thin legs, a dirt smudge below the left knee, toes curled under, a soiled short-sleeved smock, stands by the bedpost. Her mouth a straight line, her eyes dark and her short hair scraggly, she stares straight at the camera. The mustached man seated next to her looks at the camera, but his eyes are squinted. He's bare-chested, a bandanna thrown over his shoulders. Between his dungareed legs leans a young sandy-haired boy, naked but for an open striped shirt. He's the only one with his mouth open, almost smiling. He looks about to lunge from the family portrait but his father's hands hold him tightly on each arm. At the right end is an older woman, hands clutched in her lap. Only she wears worn boots and a dirty white apron. Her hair is straight, short, held behind the ears and is the same color as the bounding boy's. The floor is wood planks, as is the far wall. I can see a slit to the outside above the door and a window to the right lets in dim light.

This is some of *what is*. It's even a slight presumption to call the man the father and assume this is a family. This kind of writing takes more control and at first doesn't seem as much fun. When I started, my wild horse definitely wanted to bolt or at least to kick me in the shin. But as I kept going, I became less self-absorbed. I moved out of myself, closer to what was in front of me. But this alone—I think you can see—is a bit wooden. I'm too well behaved, dutiful, doing the assignment.

There is a tricky balance. If I remain completely outside the scene, my writing becomes a manipulation of objects, a contrived exercise. When I first began to write, I discovered that Nabokov said, "Caress the divine details." Later I read that Mies van der Rohe, the great twentieth-century architect, had pronounced, "God hides in the details." I thought, aha, so that's the key—just write details—and so I did, but my writing was stiff. I was removed and absent: the cup is on the table. The table is on the floor. The cup is white. There are two windows in the room, one on the west, one on the south side.

Then I realized why Nabokov used the verb "caress." He wanted someone's hand to touch the cup, someone's breath in the room. How am I connected to that family in the photo?

When I look again at my editor's yellow slips, the other thing she seems to repeat in different ways is: *where are you?*

Where is your response here? I feel as if you're reading
   labels on the wall. Doesn't this interest you? Challenge
   you?
What *really* do you feel?
Put yourself on the spot. Otherwise, it sounds as if you are
   copying from a textbook.
Does this have any particular resonance for *you*?

Stay with the experience.

Can you express in a way that stays closer to the *experience*?

These are simple questions. No big literary secrets here. If you don't have an editor you can ask them yourself. Here's also where reading through your practice notebooks can train you, making you alert to where you show up and where you disappear.

At the end of a weeklong workshop a student read a piece about her father eating dinner. I told her, "I liked, 'He always sat with his back to the dining room window.' "

Later at lunch she said she was surprised that I'd picked that moment out of everything. "It was odd, craggy," I said. "That's what you want with detail—not a whole string of them, but something weird or unique that you'll remember." At this point half the people at the lunch tables were turned to me, forks balanced halfway to their mouths, hands resting on water glasses. We'd been talking about concrete detail the entire week. "Oh," I laughed, "maybe I forgot to mention that. You know, when we did our simple line drawings in class, the pretty house was nice, but the person who added the TV antenna—remember? That picture made an impression.

"William Carlos Williams said you can't write about every branch on a tree. Pick the incongruous one and describe that—that will give you the whole tree.

"Think about *A Lesson Before Dying* [one of the books we had discussed in class]. It was unbearable that Jefferson was to be executed: it was huge and hung over the whole book. But Gaines had him cling to that radio—remember it playing all the time at his side? It was that offbeat detail that intensified the dread of his execution and, finally, gave Jefferson back his humanness."

The students all had looks of consternation. "It's true," I said. "After you leave here and return to Baltimore and Salt Lake City, it's the radio you'll remember—and those two old men delivering wood to the school!"

So there must be a human bond in our writing. Details alone do not work, and our human feelings unconnected to the details of the situation also do not work. What the reader is hungry for—what all readers crave—is *presence:* the writer's presence awake to the presence of the situation. I don't mean to get religious here. I'm not talking about *the* Presence, but how you, the alert, awake writer, meet the life of the scene or circumstance you're writing about. It's about life meeting life—engagement. Even if we do not personally appear in a piece, we are interacting and alive with it, somehow baring our soul as we render the soul of the story. It's a willingness to get close, but not so close we're blinded, not so close that we fail to notice detail and end up using abstract words to convey emotion—gee, the family's "suffering," the little girl is "really sad," the boy looks "so lonesome."

Writing practice taught us how to contact ourselves. Now our job, our responsibility, is to contact what's in front of us—the photo, the story, the place—and to hand that moment of contact, that merging of two presences, over to the reader.

Going back to that Walker Evans family photo, how could I enter it? That girl of eight has eyes I know. She's the one I feel closest to. I could have her tell the story of the family in first person:

Two days ago Ma fixed us oatmeal. It was good. I ate it slowly so it lasted as long as a winter fly walks across our room. Pa hasn't left for work in a long time. I'm not even sure where his blue work shirt is. My grandma used to patch it for him but now she mostly sits in the wicker chair by the window. I told li'l Andy to put on his shorts but he can never find them. I've looked for 'em too but they're nowhere.

I feel myself entering the space much more intimately when I dramatize the situation. Another approach I could use is to have the girl of eight grow up, look at the photo and write her memoir.

But then my next question is, how could I, as Natalie, stay Natalie and connect and write about this family? I probably couldn't do it right away. I can't just barge in and think: they're hungry. And then serve 'em up some brimming bowls of matzo ball soup and bagels and lox. I'd have to sink in, discover their longing for corn bread, black-eyed peas, maybe collard greens. I'd have to find an entry point. Some place where my life met theirs. I might have to read more about Alabama, 1936, where and when this photo was shot. Or my access might come through reading more about Walker Evans, the artist who took the photo.

All this requires work, exertion. We each carry an essential life force, but to contact it, to glow with our being—free of opinion, philosophy, idea—and meet the clear life in others takes tremendous effort. This is where we call on the power of those two years of writing practice. Then we can throw ourselves into the world— and into the craggy, odd, empathic true life of a writer.

THAT SMALL COLORADO TOWN

TWELVE YEARS AGO I received a phone call from a woman named Dolores: would I come up to San Luis and speak to a weekly writers' group?

Writers were meeting there? In that small Colorado town near the border, north of Taos? I was tired—I'd been traveling and teaching too much—but this offer was too hard to turn down. I'd been drawn to that historic Spanish town, the oldest in the state, for a long time. Right off Main Street was a crucifix walk up the bare mountain behind the thin strip of buildings and stores. A tourist or a native could stop at the twelve stations of the cross as they climbed on the path and simultaneously be renewed by the beauty of the San Luis Valley that spread out before them. The place had seemed foreign and impenetrable to me; yet, in my novel Nell had stopped there on her return to New Mexico and even had an epiphany on their sidewalk as she ran her finger along the window of a second-hand shop.

We'll make you a potluck dinner, Dolores proposed on the other end of the phone.

How could I refuse?

The next Wednesday my friend Judith and I made the hour-long drive up. The road was lined with wild sunflowers bobbing their heads in the late August heat. We found the house on a small side road among Russian olives. Shadows were deep just before twilight. The living room felt crowded with big stuffed chairs. Lace curtains hung at the windows and doilies padded the soft sofa. The sun set outside but still, few lamps were lit indoors, making the room dim and muted. I had a plate of enchiladas, rice, a tamale, a piece of corn on the cob and salad on my lap. Eight or nine writers sat around. I looked across at Judith and could tell she was enjoying herself, chatting with our hosts, a bit amazed to be in someone's home in San Luis. It was clear that no one really wanted me to talk about writing. They simply wanted to socialize. I wondered what I was doing there.

Dessert was served. I helped myself to a slice of homemade coffee cake, two biscocitos and an almond cookie. I looked at my plate and was about to ask myself how I would eat all this, when a man in black leather, with long, dark, scraggly hair and a full beard, exploded through the door. My head jerked up. I was sure he was in the wrong place—I wanted to say, "The Hell's Angels are down the block." But everyone called out, "Hey, Leon."

I forgot about dessert. Was he in this group? He carried a pile of notebooks, disheveled folders full of typed manuscripts, and he plopped himself in front of me. "You gotta help me. What do I do with all this?"

I didn't hesitate. "Read me something." Everyone gathered round.

I can't remember the exact story now, but it was full of energy. This man lived on the page. But he also needed reams of editing and direction.

He told me he had been brought up in this town and lived here all his life. He worked nights shelving cans and boxes in the small grocery, so that he could have all day to write.

You can go to workshops, to universities, to learn the craft of writing. But to learn the spirit of writing—where do you go? This man had the thing that was hard to learn. I glanced at his writing pile. No, I didn't have time to direct his work but I suddenly had an idea. "Judith will read one of your manuscripts for you!" I turned to Judith. "Would you?" I knew this wasn't fair. She was a long-time student of mine and a friend.

I think Judith was so taken with the evening she said, "Sure," without hesitation. He handed a folder right over. "Careful, it's my only copy." I gulped.

On the ride home I apologized to Judith. I told her I'd help, if she didn't want to look at all of it.

"No, really, I'm curious."

"It haunts me," I told her. "I got lucky and found an editor who helps me with craft. Really, I'm more like Leon—all I knew was writing practice. You contact your soul, but it gives you no finesse. Sure, I've learned on my own a lot about refining, but there comes a point when you can't do it alone. Writing is handed on person to person. Who will Leon find?"

A week later Judith told me he had some real high points and then pages and pages of repetition and fill-in that would have to go. She wrote him a letter and sent back the manuscript. He called and thanked her.

Through the years I thought of him. Last summer I drove through San Luis on my way to Boulder. On impulse I stopped and parked my car. The grocery was still there. I walked in—it was late morning. At that point I didn't even remember his name—how could I ask about him?

I walked to the back of the store. There was an open swinging door. I saw a large empty space and shelves further back. This must be the warehouse, I thought. I stepped through.

Across the room a clean-shaven man with glasses noticed me. He saw my awkwardness and walked over. "I'm looking for a man who writes—" I began.

"Are you the author? I thought I recognized you."

"It's you? You're still here?"

"I own the place now. Do you have a moment? Come to my office."

I followed him past the rows of vinegar and oil, past the stacked bags of lumpy brown sugar.

"Do you still write?" We settled into gray metal chairs. Now that he was a store owner maybe he had quit.

"Oh, yeah," he smiled broadly. "I'm working on a novel about a priest. You know, someone heard about me and I was invited to a Chicano writers' festival at the University of Colorado last year. I was on stage with Tony Anaya and some other big shots. I thought, oh boy, what am I doing here? But when I read everyone loved it— they really did. Now the word's out and I've been invited to Jackson Hole this summer."

I smiled broadly. So spirit can carry us a long way, I thought. Even if work is rough and needs a lot of attention, we can feel something. We say, hey, he's a storyteller, we can't stop reading— or listening. This kind of writing with spark, energy, presence attracts other writers and editors, who are willing to go out on a limb and who want to help.

And we all need help.

ENLIGHTENMENT OR THE PULITZER?

MAYBE YOU'VE FIGURED OUT how to focus your writing. Maybe your pages are alive with energy and spirit. But wait—there's more. If you decide to write a book—to commit to a long project—how can you keep the juice flowing?

I posed this question in an ongoing writing group that met periodically. These were people working on essays, short stories, novels. They knew what it was like to try to keep going.

Lorraine raised her hand. "Last spring after the workshop was over I decided my characters were boring, there was nothing redeeming. I put it all away, decided it was a failure and didn't touch it all summer. Then this morning at eight Natalie called me. She asked me to bring in something from my novel to read in the first class.

" 'Sure,' I said. 'I have plenty to choose from.'

"Then I spent the next seven hours—except for the quickest shower I ever took—till three o'clock when we started class, going over my chapters. I really liked it again and I even jotted down a whole summary." She was beaming.

I turned to the class: "Now what's important about what she said? What clue does this give us about continuing and staying connected to our work?"

"She wrote a synopsis," one student offered.

I shook my head.

"She was judgmental of her work and now she isn't!" another student chimed in.

"Naa," I said, "we're always up and down." I paused. "What kept her going?"

No answer.

"I called her! Someone cared! Someone reached out and shook her awake."

Sometimes by ourselves we can get lost, especially when it's all coming from us. It's important to have a friend who is intensely interested in your project, who knows your characters and the story you are trying to tell. That friend listens to your woes and complaints, bolsters up your flagging ego. I have usually found that friend to be another writer—he or she can relate. But the other person does not always have to be a fellow writer. Then you have the luxury of not reversing roles, not being the compassionate listener to another beleaguered writer who is also trying to wrestle with some unpalpable immensity—lost love, night, insanity—and get it on the page. This is diffcrent from a critique group where you bring in finished work and people comment. This friend is someone who takes pleasure in what you are doing. Remember that word: pleasure. The secret is: we writers love to be cared about and we love our writing. No greater delight than to talk about it, to be asked about it.

I have a future novel in mind about a young woman named Yolanda. My friend Eddie never lets me forget her. We're sitting in a luncheonette watching a woman across the room stuff her purse with straws and then take the cap off the mustard and chug down a big yellow glob. Eddie leans over the table to me. "That's something Yo might do."

Yeah, I think—and get all excited again about my future book.

Whenever my friend Ted Ringer was stuck writing *Get Outta Town,* he'd go down to the local bar—half his characters hung out there—and ask them what they thought should happen next. They'd throw out some absurd ideas—"Hey, why don't you have them steal a spaceship"—and Ted would nod, jot something down on a napkin, go home and try it. It kept things lively. He had the pleasure of other people interested and feeding his work.

I ask Eddie, "So, is there a lesbian in your book?"

He shakes his head, "No, but I'll consider it."

When Katagiri Roshi was still alive, I taught a benefit writing retreat at Hokyoji, his monastery in southeastern Minnesota near New Albin, Iowa. On Friday thirty students were arriving from all over the country. I hung out by the winding Winnebago Creek, so happy to be near the red barns and the bluffs of the Mississippi. As the students arrived, they came down to greet me. I jokingly asked each one, "So which do you want more, enlightenment or the Pulitzer?"

Each and every one shot back, "Enlightenment!"

"Fools, fools," I told them in class the next day. "I'd much rather win the Pulitzer"—even though I was the only Buddhist there. As the week went on we continued to challenge each other: quick, if you could only have one for the rest of your life, which would you choose: sex or laughter? The country or the city? Then this one: would you rather be blind, deaf and mute or have five million dollars?—now that one really stopped us in our tracks. Steve Abbott—a fine writer from San Francisco—made that one up. He had a wonderful mind. He died of AIDS eight years later. When I heard he was gone, I was sad. He wrote from the raw edge of his thoughts. I salute him now.

Anyway, it is twelve years from that time in the humid midwestern June heat and I wonder about my original question. What was it I was asking by that slow river? I think it was, what is our direction? Enlightenment is a large diffuse thing—it has no trajectory. Better to aim for something concrete. When I hear people who write beautifully yet for years never publish a poem, attempt an essay or dare to put their work in a form, I want to inquire, what is it we have to say, where is our urgency, our burning?

I have advocated long and hard to my students, please, please, give yourself some space. Don't be so product oriented. But there does come a time—I can't honestly tell you when—that we must step over the line of practice and speak and expect to be heard. But no one's listening, we whine. Then we have to figure out how to make them listen. It's not their fault. It's our responsibility to give vitality, muscle, movement to our words. I have incited everyone to do writing practice and now I'm saying, let's kick ass.

When do we begin? As Hemingway said, "Not too soon, but not too damn much after."

TRUE NELL

PEOPLE ASK ME: do you use writing practice when you work on a book?

I smile. It's the only thing I know. I use it as the ground of all my writing.

When I worked on *Banana Rose* I'd sit down at a table, open my notebook and say, OK, now, this chapter begins with Nell in Fort Collins. By the time it ends she has to be in Nebraska. Go for two hours. I'd have a backbone structure—a trip from one state to another—but I didn't know how she'd get there. Sure, it was a car—Nell didn't own a plane or a hot air balloon—but her journey would be revealed as I wrote. That is the adventure of writing, it is an act of discovery. If I knew everything she'd do beforehand, I would be bored sick and never keep writing. However, I didn't let her turn the car around and suddenly head for California—two chapters later I needed her in Minnesota. But she could think about going to Arizona or Nevada as her car aimed for the heart of the Midwest. She could even make a wrong turn and drive toward Wyoming, but then she'd have to get back on track. This was the fun—how many stops did she make? How many candy wrappers were strewn on the car floor? Having secure boundaries—Colorado to Nebraska—gave the freedom to dig deep into possibility. Without that structure Nell could get lost for a long time—head down to Mexico, South America and out of my story forever.

But of course that wouldn't have been true Nell. Her heart was tied to a man's in the Twin Cities—her freedom lay in playing out her life, her karma, the cards she was dealt. As a writer, the more I could step away and let true Nell come through, the more I could relax into her unfolding and let her take her proper place in the universe. I could not manipulate her—that I learned painfully in the first year of writing that book. She had her own way and she would live it or I would not get a novel at all. This was true for all the characters in the book.

But that doesn't mean I was out of control. I could throw in a monkey wrench, a flat tire, a roadblock and see what Nell would do. I could test her, challenge her, scare her, but Nell was Nell. Her essence lived on its own.

But where on its own, you ask? After all, you created her. Wasn't she in your imagination?

I guess so, but once I set her spinning she became a living entity. You could never physically shake her hand, but she existed nevertheless in some alternate universe. What is imagination anyway? Nobody owns it—it is outside, beyond our physical limitations, larger than our limited concept of ourselves, where everything is created out of exquisite chaos. A writer reaches out and grabs some of that mess and creates form through words.

But this sounds too magical. I pick up my pen and direct writing practice down a certain road, riverbed, gully. When I use this method I have a bigger world, with more possibilities moving through me, than if I just try to create out of my own small mind with its strong ideas about how something should be.

I also use writing practice to revise my work. For instance, I re-read a chapter I'd written a week earlier: hmm, I need to develop that brown hat Gauguin is wearing. I put an A in a circle next to the hat. Then I take a blank piece of paper, put a circled A on top, and say to myself, "OK, go for ten minutes, brown hat."

By returning to writing practice, I can get faster, hotter takes on Brown Hat than if I tried to conjure up some idea from my self-conscious brain. Let's see, *big* brown hat? No, I cross out "big." Nice? Interesting? Oh, I have it! Fat brown hat. Naa. Instead we need to let it rip, let it come from out back, off the head, around the neck, out the ear. Otherwise we'll be pondering Brown Hat till our eyes water and we fall asleep.

But does everything in our book have to be alive? Why not? We don't want our reader falling asleep alongside us.

LUNCH WITH THE EDITOR

I REMEMBER HEADING DOWN Fifth Avenue and thinking: writer gets to go out with her editors in New York. What more could I want! We went to a restaurant around the corner from the Bantam offices. The moment we swung through the doors, we were greeted by platters of bright mangoes and oranges, rounds of Parmesan cheese, twisted golden breads, strawberry tortes, and rich éclairs piled high on a mahogany table. Waiters flew by with tall-throated glasses held on trays at shoulder height. We were hurried through the crowd to our reserved table in the center of the room. When we settled in our seats I didn't want to speak, just to look around and absorb the tailored navy suits, careful mouths of dark lipstick, intense faces leaning across twenty-four-dollar salads to converse in fast, clipped sentences. You felt deals were being made and by dessert vacation plans to small unknown countries were being shared.

I had been brought up an hour from the city by the Long Island Railroad, but this was not my New York. As adolescents my sister and I had drifted down Thirty-fourth Street, peered into store win-

184

dows, spooned coffee ice cream into our mouths among the old ladies in dark booths at Schrafft's, crooked our necks at neon in Times Square, and then tumbled down the staircases in Penn Station heading home, exhausted from hours of indecision and arguing about whether to go to the Village or Central Park.

Over appetizers my editors leaned in to share publishing gossip, especially about a male model who appeared barechested on the covers of many romance novels. I had never heard of him. Then we actually talked about the weather. I knew this was not just polite conversation. New Yorkers are great walkers. Rain matters, wind, snow, sudden clouds are all studied through glass windows during work hours. Will they need an umbrella, snowshoes, a scarf, a hat? Can they walk the twenty blocks to meet a friend this evening, should they hail a cab or rush to a subway station?

The main dishes were served. I had salmon in a pastry puff. The first three bites were delicious. I was easing into euphoria when they both turned to me. "Now let's discuss the manuscript." Suddenly I lost my appetite. I lowered my fork onto the edge of the plate.

I knew that for Toni and Linda this was simply a matter-of-fact discussion. This is what they did for a living. We were talking about typed words on a white page and how to improve them. I held tight to my chair and made an earnest effort to listen. These two women were savvy. They had good things to say. But I felt as though I were sitting stark naked in a perfectly civilized eating establishment. At that moment, the important thing for me to understand was that naked Natalie was none of their business. I had to take care of her.

Imagine how many books editors work on. If they had to administer to each writer's wounds and woes, they'd have to build a mile-wide mental institution. Toni and Linda were not saying, Natalie, you are an idiot, a moron, because the third chapter needs to be developed. Their comments had nothing to do with me personally—with how I looked, dressed, my hygiene, whether I was popular back in high school, or whether my parents were rich, who I married, if I donated to nonprofits, or shopped ecologically. They only suggested in concise terms that I explain more clearly what I meant in chapter eight that would link it to the result in chapter ten.

My hope is that I teach a steady way of listening through writing practice. No good, no bad, I tell my students. When we listen to each other's work, we are studying mind: not evaluating it, not judging it, just listening. I want to develop in students that large mind that accepts and does not cling. I tell them if we can accept others' writing as they read aloud, we can also accept our own. This practice creates a strong spine, so that we are not tossed away by criticism. And actually no editor I've ever worked with has passed judgment on my writing. Instead they explained how to make it better or told me I hadn't quite connected yet, I had to go back to the drawing board.

Naturally, the writing does come from us—it grows in us and is nourished by our bodies—but it's also our responsibility to cut the umbilical cord. No writer I know fails to experience the wrench of separation, but it's important to go on and let the manuscript live on its own out there in the playing fields of the world.

Last winter I worked hard on baking a perfect cranberry pie. My friend took his first bite. His face puckered up.

"Bitter?" I asked.

"You forgot the sugar," he grimaced.

Nat, you forgot the plot. Nat, you forgot the action. At times I've even forgotten where the book was going, why I was writing it and who I was anyway. But this pie wasn't baked yet. It could be fixed. Toni and Linda were trying to help. They had flour on their fists.

And that day at lunch, I tried to help them—even though my clothes were torn off—by shutting up and simply listening. DO NOT TAKE IT PERSONALLY!—make that a practice. Even though it may feel personal, it is words on a page. Though I felt exposed, they weren't talking about me.

But I'll tell you a secret: after lunch, after I said good-bye to Linda and Toni, I walked straight down to Macy's on Thirty-fourth Street. I wandered down the aisles touching sweaters and scarves. My mother had worked there behind the Richard Hudnut counter selling the Dubarry line of cosmetics in her twenties when her hair was long, wavy, thick and black and her dark eyes flashed. I still wore her gold clip-on earrings from those days. "Mom," I whispered, fingering a pink angora hat, "I'm a writer. I just met with my editors. Mom, they were smart and they liked my work." I reached for a pair of wool mittens. "Someday I promise I'll write about you." Macy's had never been so comforting. My clothes returned to my body and my worlds came together.

CLEAN YOUR DISHES

AFTER I READ THROUGH Linda's first comments on my manuscript, I phoned her. Though I loved Linda, she was only twenty-seven, only recently promoted to editor. What could she teach me? A lot. Linda splayed me open with her red pen. "Linda," I asked her, "how do you know so much?"

She paused a moment, then said a brilliant thing: "I use my wild mind to edit. I drop away, enter your mind and move through your writing. What is Natalie trying to do, to say? I pull you out, make you clearer."

While Linda was editing *Banana Rose,* she'd queried me every time my characters ate a meal: "Well, who's clearing the dishes?" I was still green and excited and so for the first half of the novel I responded dutifully. I had Nell scrape the dinner dishes and Gauguin heat up the sudsy water. Who knew? Maybe cleaning dishes had some heavy literary connotation all the way back to Chaucer. Then one morning it struck me like lightning; I bolted from the library table and dashed outside to the pay phone—I can still feel the cold metal against my ear. "Linda, weren't you the youngest in your family? I bet you had the job of clearing the table."

I could feel her astonishment all the way from the twentieth floor in mid-Manhattan. "How did you know?"

"You told me. When you let loose your wild mind on my manuscript, you disclosed it. It took me a while to catch on!"

After that I understood the intimacy of writer and editor in a whole new way. Someone who edits your work—at any level—is giving you their mind, just as in your writing you have given them yours. Mind-to-mind transmission.

Toni has told me how she paces when she is about to open a new manuscript, how she is nervous, excited, scared. Even after thirty years, she says, plunging in has not gotten any easier.

That early spring through late summer I worked hard. I'd finish the revisions, send them in. To my great disbelief, Linda sent them back each time—her wild mind combed through them. I'd crawl again to the Harwood Library, watch beautiful weather pass me by out the high windows. I felt as if I'd been held back a year to finish my fourth-grade composition—what the American flag means to me. I was too young to carry so much. Surely, they'd let me out for recess—life can't continue this way.

Linda suggests that I get rid of an entire chapter. It's about Mrs. Montoya, a chicken who becomes enlightened. Even the coyotes don't eat her: they carry her away only so they can be near her.

"Absolutely not," I say at first. I love that chapter! I begin to enumerate its brilliant points.

"I'd cut it out," she repeats.

I wrestle with it, even though by now I know she's right. The chapter slows down the movement of the story, but I don't want to let it go. I spend three days trying to make it work. On the fourth day, I sit at my desk, and groan, "Nat, it's eating you up." I ax it out and my muscles fall back on my bones again.

There's another chapter I love. I'm certain it's the best one in the book. Nell goes to see *Tender Mercies* eight times and at the last show sings aloud "Wings of a Dove" along with Robert Duvall. At Linda's request I do a little research and find out that the movie came out two years after the novel ends!

"The chapter has to go," Linda says.

"No, not that one," I whine. "Does it matter that much? Come on, how important can it be? No one will care."

I sigh, such a little detail. Such a great chapter.

I'll show Linda, I decide one day alone in the middle of my miserable morning. I'll publish those two chapters separately in magazines. Both of them will be chosen for *Best Short Stories of 1996*. The movie rights will be sold for the "Enlightened Chicken." When I go on my book tour I'll only read The Chapters That Did Not Make It.

Three weeks later I look at those two chapters again and discover they don't matter to me anymore. They've been cut from the bloodline. The novel is what matters. I am in service to the novel.

As fall approaches I work on the last pages. I call Eddie on the phone: "Quick—give me another word for 'then.' I'm burned out."

I call Linda, "Just help me with the last paragraphs. I can't do this anymore." I was reduced to begging.

I wanted to turn to the sleeping old man at the next library table or call my mother in Florida, "Please write these last words for me."

I imagine my mother would say, "Natli is a sweet girl—tell them that."

I'd write it down on the last page of the manuscript. "Thank you, Mom. You just made it the great American novel."

"Anytime, darling."

I'd breathe deeply. Someone had come to my rescue.

I sent in the manuscript and called Toni Burbank. "I physically can't lift my pen. I couldn't do another revision if my life depended on it."

She laughed. "I guess we've gotten everything we could out of you. We editors make bets around here—how much do you think we can wring from this one?"

Friends treated me like a leper at the time—"There she goes with her novel." What I didn't say and didn't fully understand is that I was pushed beyond anything I'd thought I was capable of. I've done hundred-day training periods—up each morning at four, twenty degrees below zero, six blocks to walk down back alleys to the Minnesota Zen Center. Those days at the Harwood were harder.

I tell my students, "If you know someone who's writing a novel, take them out for lunch. If they've finished one, even if it never gets published, it's a great feat and a huge sustained effort. Bring them flowers."

My students laugh.

I say I'm not kidding.

DRINK A CUP OF TEA

LAST MAY I WORKED with a small group of old students. Rarely in class do I comment very much on students' work. Mostly I try to create a space where they can step forward with whatever they've written and build confidence in their voice. But this group was different. They'd all studied with me for at least two years and it seemed time for me to remark on their direction. They evidently wanted it—they'd signed up for this week, traveled from long distances, brought manuscripts to go over. Yet from the first session on, the tension in the room was so thick I could hardly breathe. During each meeting at least two mature women would burst out crying. They feared what I would say and my gentlest comments were taken wrong. When I made a joke it fell to the ground like a lead pancake.

At one point I commented that coincidentally the two books we had read were both about a relationship between two men.

"What?" one of the students asked.

I repeated myself.

She became frustrated. "I don't get it. What?"

I said it one more time.

"What do you mean?" She was wringing her hands.

"Really, Susan, I'm not saying anything that deep. In Don Kurtz's book there were two men." I held up two fingers. "In Monette's book—two." I nodded reassuringly.

"Explain it to me." Her face was bright red and her voice was a shrill, desperate whine.

"Please!" . . . and then I flashed on the zendo in Minnesota. Katagiri would say something simple—"The present moment is right here," or "When you drink a cup of tea, pay attention to drinking a cup of tea"—and we strained to understand its supernatural, profound and enlightened intent. We were so self-conscious, so tense, so earnest that we missed everything. If he said, "This is a hand," we construed it to mean a foot, an elbow, the suffering of Bodhidharma.

After my week of teaching was over, I felt bewildered. Jean Leyshon, my assistant who is also a Zen monk, was sitting at my kitchen table. We had paperwork to do, but I couldn't concentrate. Finally, I interrupted our work and told her about the tension in the workshop.

She listened quietly, then paused, her face lit up. "It's wonderful that your students were willing to experience such fear. It's rare that we let ourselves feel pure fear and then sit with it for a whole week. Tremendous!"

So when someone edits your work—in class or privately—you should be stalwart but also let yourself bristle with pure fear! Let it ripple through your whole body, let it burn you to a crisp like a marshmallow—it's another way to be done with yourself. Then you can listen like a rock or a mountain when someone tells you, "This feels like grinding it out—you're reciting by rote. This image isn't earning its way each time you use it. These pages don't make it."

Beethoven Practiced Too

DURING THAT WEEK IN MAY when I worked with my old students, I handed out sheets of sentences lifted from my original manuscripts. I asked them to see if they could make the sentences stronger, more concise, less clunky.

Here are some of them, followed by the revisions my editors had suggested.

> And I got the idea of what artistic was from *New Yorker* covers and from the cartoon drawings inside.
> *My idea of "artistic" came from* New Yorker *covers and from the cartoon drawings inside.*

> I snatched the photo away from her and lifted out of my pack an old *Southwest Art* magazine with paintings by Barbara inside. I flipped open to "Fall in the Canyon."
> *I snatched the photo away from her and lifted an old* Southwest Art *magazine out of my pack. I flipped it open to Barbara's "Fall in the Canyon."*

The dumber I got the better, then I wouldn't approach a
painting with fancy art theories. I wanted to have a direct
connection with the painting before me.

*The dumber I got the better. I didn't want fancy art theories. I
wanted a direct connection with the painting before me.*

Lil was known for her notorious long legs.

Lil was notorious for her long legs.

I had to have a willingness to paint really ugly pictures.

I had to be willing to paint really ugly pictures.

When my sister and I received baby chicks for Passover that
we named Ginger and Daisy, Grandpa cared for them in
the garage as they grew older and we were no longer
interested.

*One year my sister and I received baby chicks for Passover. We lost
interest in them soon after we named them Ginger and Daisy, but
Grandpa cared for them in the garage.*

I hadn't taken off my wool coat, just unbuttoned it. It was
navy.

I hadn't taken off my navy wool coat, just unbuttoned it.

I was outside. It was night and cold and it was a great relief.

I was outside. The cold night air was a great relief.

We took a hike in a nearby birch forest. One tree duplicated
the one next to it for mile after mile.

*We hiked in a nearby birch forest where one tree duplicated the next
for mile after mile.*

"What's goin' on here?" the officer asked in a southern
accent.

"What's goin' on here?" the officer drawled.

I said to the students, "Do you see how the sentences move more smoothly, are more efficient, but how the editors at the same time kept the integrity of my own words and mostly changed the structure?"

I was astonished once again by the group. They liked revising the sentences, but that wasn't what they really found beneficial.

"You're a fuck-up just like the rest of us," one of them piped up, grinning ear to ear.

"Of course, you know that. I've told you countless stories—remember the one where I actually fell asleep over my own boring, tedious sentences? And what about the writing practices I've read in class? They haven't all been ace wonders of the universe."

"Yeah, but we've been trained not to judge writing practice—we just accepted yours. You've *told* us about your screw-ups, but you never *showed* us."

Then another student slapped the hand-out sheet. "But here's living proof. You handed these sentences in?" He shook his head in mock disapproval.

"Yes I did." I dilated my nostrils and pursed my lips. "And my Toni and my Linda were kinder than you sharks." I glanced at the clock. "Ahh, it's dinnertime. Class dismissed. I hope they have something miserable for you to eat."

Nothing could dampen their elation.

Later on I realized what had happened. Reading a book, listening to a symphony, seeing paintings in a museum—these are all done deals. They seem monolithic, complete unto themselves. How was it done? No, it wasn't done; like Athena it sprang complete from Zeus's head.

Once at the Pierpont Morgan Library I saw working manuscripts of Beethoven, Mozart, Brahms, Liszt and Tchaikovsky. I was stunned. They were full of cross-outs and revisions—you mean these composers were human beings? Mozart's Fortieth Symphony didn't come straight from the realm of the gods? Seeing those scores was a huge experience for me, an opening—these were people who had to think, work, listen, hear, go back over. They experienced human need and desire, an urge to create, the longing for beauty and wholeness. I know this seems naive—that I didn't realize this before, but I didn't. I'd broken the code in painting and writing, but my experience didn't translate to music, and a concert remained magical to me. Perhaps, if I consciously thought of it, I might have surmised that those symphonies I heard at Lincoln Center vibrating through catgut and human breath came from real people, but sitting in a room filled with sound I still wouldn't have believed it. I had to be shown those handwritten scores.

For my students, gloating was a victory. They'd seen a chink in the monopoly published authors held for them. Writing practice had given them the "in" on how to write, but a finished book was still outside the mortal realm. Mistakes made the endeavor human.

THE THICK RED BOOK

FOR YEARS BY MYSELF I took my writing practices and tried to go the next step: to make them sleek and lovely. I wanted each sentence to work with the one before it. What was clunky? What felt off? It wasn't immediately apparent. I'd read the words aloud, comb the verbiage, stumble on the knots. I developed an inner ear. If something was off my eardrum almost twitched, a signal to zoom in and scrutinize the lines. Sometimes I couldn't find the problem right away—but the twitch was never wrong! So I looked more closely:

> I can see mouse tracks in the snow at my feet and a tiny line where its tail scored the snow. I hear the crunch of my galoshes through the crusted, lavender snow. In the distance the freeway is humming with Christmas shoppers and red-wing blackbirds are flying across the swamp.

Good sentences—not mine, Brett Gadbois's, an old friend—but what's off? "Snow" is in there three times, in two sentences; the repetition creates a slight drag. How can I get rid of this excess baggage?

I can see mouse tracks at my feet and a tiny line where its tail scored the snow. I hear the crunch of my galoshes through the lavender crust. In the distance the freeway is humming with Christmas shoppers and red-wing blackbirds are flying across the swamp.

Sometimes it's not so easy to ax out the word and have it work. Then I have to find other words for snow that enhance the text, rather than using the same word and causing redundancy. My friend John Thorndike told me about the *Synonym Finder* by J. I. Rodale (Warner Books) four years ago. Every time I write I use that heavy paperback at least eight times. My crimson copy is worn and I've bought many others for friends. Let's say I need an alternative for "brown." I look it up: thirty-eight to choose from, including chestnut, coffee, roan, rust, auburn, sorrel, brick. What pleasure!

My weeklong May workshop ended at noon on a Sunday. A few students had to leave early that morning to catch a plane in Albuquerque and would miss the last class.

"C'est dommage," I teased. "It is then I plan to tell the true secret of writing."

"What? What?" They threw up their hands and begged.

"The thick red book," I whispered and slipped out the door.

SLOW WALKING

ONE THING THAT HAS HELPED ME stay simple, elemental, grounded in my writing is slow walking practice. Sometimes I'll feel frantic and complicated—I can't possibly write the book I said I would. Then that thought multiplies: what! are you crazy! Who do you think you are anyway? I become frightened, impotent, small. My project is a mighty force like an army tank about to flatten me.

Nat, let's take a walk, I say to myself. A long walk.

But this is not a fast walk, using that frenetic energy for aerobics. Instead we have all the time in the world, one foot after the other. The walk is not a hike; I might just circumambulate my room. I probably look like a zombie, but I'm not in a trance; I'm actually paying very close attention to my feet. I'm feeling my right foot flex—those adorable toes spreading, the light spongy mass of my heel lifting, my weight shifting to the left side. Then I sense my knee bending, my right hip dropping, my body falling forward as I move my foot a small space above the floor, then settle it on the ground again. As I slow down, space becomes immense, time is huge. Lifting, bending, placing—who am I? In this unhurried, compassionate life, what is it I want to say?

Certainly, I am capable of anything, even the book—and it's not a book anymore, it's one day after another, sitting down and writing. The writing accumulates. I take another holy step—the world comes home to me. I want to tell about the soup I ate that cold Wednesday last winter. I want to write about the jackrabbit that came down the chimney into my studio. His tawny thick fur, his feral yellow eyes are alive to me all over again in the slow motion of my step.

If I am going to write at a café, I park a distance away, so I can walk there slowly. During that walk I drop the argument I had with my lover, the bill I didn't pay, my car that needs an oil change. I am aiming for my notebook, my pen, the open page, the beginning of Part II. But I don't think about Part II. I hold it in my belly. My words will come out when I arrive at the corner table and I will write them in pen in a notebook. My hand attached to my arm, shoulder, chest, will move across the page and feel connected to my heart, where I want the work to emerge.

But what about computers? I am often asked. Pressing keys is a different physical activity from writing by hand. A slightly different angle of mind comes out, not better or worse, only different. But, I tell my students, don't ever lose your ability to hand-write— someday you may not be able to pay your electric bill or you'll be in the woods by a stream and want to write, or like me, at a library or café. Even though we drive a car, we can't forget how to walk. The same is true with a computer. It's still good to stay in touch with the clutch of a pen and the texture of paper.

I rarely think about a book I'm working on. To think too much about it while I'm not physically working on it usually means to worry, to toss around discursive ideas. The real writing comes from the abdomen, from my whole body in the act of writing it. Usually when I'm working on one book my monkey mind is playing with the book it *really* wants to write: the next one. "Oh, Nat, quit or finish this already, will you?" My mind is full of enthusiasm for the book on Paris, she's certain it will be a smash hit. She thinks I'm tedious working day after day on the manuscript at hand. I give this restless one, this toddler, some toys to play with: a small plastic Eiffel Tower, a beret, a photo of the Seine. "Here, darling, sit quietly in the corner." She rarely is quiet, but at least she has her own activity. "Can't you feel it?" she asks. "Pierre is stroking Madeleine's arm as they sit, eating croissants in the Luxembourg Gardens. He bends to kiss her, their lips touch, crumbs fall to their laps."

While she is occupied in France, she frees me up to drop deep into the world of the work before me.

I read an article by Lawrence Shainberg about athletes training for the "zone." The zone is a special place that opens up at moments of peak performance. In the middle of fast action and pressure—in basketball or soccer, say—everything slows down. The players feel calm, clear, confident. How do they prepare for this? Their coaching includes reading a book while watching television. One young Olympic archer practiced wearing earphones, listening to the radio as she shot her arrows. All this increased concentration.

I think connecting with the slow movement of my feet and the realization of space and also having my monkey mind occupied with my future book works the same way. It decreases my fear and increases my concentration for the book at hand. This is also why I write in cafés. The more activity in the restaurant the better—juke-

box blasting, phone ringing, cook calling out orders—more enter-
tainment for monkey mind, leaving deep mind to do its task.

I tell my students: writing is a physical activity. I happen to be a
great athlete, even though you don't see my muscles. I'm training for The Zone—along with Michael Jordan, Pelé, and Jackie
Joyner-Kersee.

I'm Tired

FIVE YEARS AGO IN DENVER I sat meditation with a Buddhist teacher who was visiting from Cambridge. His lectures made Zen koans very alive for me. At the retreat we studied Case Seventy-three from the *Blue Cliff Record*. Each morning he read the entire koan to us and then talked about it. Here is part of the koan:

A monk asked Grand Master Ma, "Please, Teacher, going beyond the permutations of assertion and denial, directly point out to me the meaning of the coming from the West."

Master Ma said, "I'm tired today and can't explain for you. Go ask Chih Tsang."

When the monk asked Chih Tsang, Tsang said, "Why didn't you ask the Teacher?" The monk said, "The Teacher had me come here to ask you." Tsang said, "I have a headache today and can't explain for you. Go ask Elder Brother Hai."

Each time he read the koan I listened intently, but I never even tried to understand or penetrate it. Then one evening the whole situation seemed perfectly obvious. The Zen master *was really* tired. It wasn't a trick, some esoteric Asian puzzle. Through days of sitting my complicated mind suddenly unraveled enough to realize this. My thinking had to become flat: a glass of water was a glass of water. I didn't need to realize the hugeness of the Pacific in the glass, just to allow things to be as they are. Can you imagine a crow cawing and then evaluating it? Was that loud enough? Did I sound good?

As I sat the whole thing sank into me. The Zen master sends the neophyte to ask the senior student, but when he goes to him the senior student says, I can't help you now, I have a terrible headache. Well, by god, he had a headache! He probably was working too hard to answer his own koan and his head was throbbing.

Recently I read a reference in the *Book of Serenity:* "Like pouring milk into milk." That is a beautiful image—can you imagine it? When you're done, you cannot distinguish the first glass of milk from the second. No separation. When the Zen master said he was tired—it was a hundred percent! It filled the world. No space for meaning anything else. The same with the headache. A good headache bangs through your whole brain—there is not a moment in which you don't have a headache.

I sat there with my mind leveled, deflated, open.

Can we write this way? "She walked in the room." No counter-motive. Let the story unfold by itself. Write one pure statement—and then another. Don't cover up, backslide, explain. "I wanted a motorcycle." Don't be ashamed or worried you'll appear macho or weird.

Tell the plain truth. Taking one step after another, arrive in the center of your writing.

EPILOGUE:
A WRITING RETREAT

LAST MARCH I SUBLET AN APARTMENT from a friend in Mill Valley, California. I'd seen his place two years before—a flat on the second floor of an old house with a porch overlooking a vegetable garden and Monterey pines jagged and dark in the distance—and I'd known right away I wanted to stay there sometime. I loved the old linoleum in the kitchen and the living room window looking down on a trellis covered with pale pink roses. It was all so different from my dry New Mexico. I wanted to know about rain again, fog, mist, damp doorknobs and steamy mornings. I called him a year later and asked if he was going away for any length of time. I think he was surprised—in his swanky town his place was considered a bit dilapidated. But I am drawn to what is funky, slightly unkempt, a tad shabby—growth and human life seem more possible there.

He said, yes, he'd be gone in the spring—and could I water his plants? Who knew that March, muddy from snowmelt and windy in my home state, is the heavenly moment in the Bay Area—everything at its quintessential opening—lilacs, first hawthorn, bridal veil, wild crab apple.

I have many good friends around Marin County. I told myself I'd do a writing "retreat," but, in truth, I figured I'd write a little, socialize a lot, climb Mount Tam, frequent good restaurants, drive often into the city to go to concerts and readings, and to browse through bookstores.

I landed late on a Tuesday afternoon, rented a purple Suzuki from a rude rental agent, and wove my way driving for the first time through San Francisco, petrified of the steep streets, making a wrong turn off Van Ness and accidentally heading for the crookedest street in America, frantically looking for the entrance to Highway 101, which would take me over the Golden Gate Bridge to Marin.

It was dusk when I finally arrived in Mill Valley. I quickly unpacked and fell into an exhausted sleep. When I woke Wednesday morning, to my surprise I realized I meant business about this retreat. I charged over to the library, found out the hours and coordinated my writing with that schedule. I needed an outside structure to dictate my routine. In relying on that I could fall more deeply into the notebook without diversion.

That first day my mind was agitated. I had twenty-one days before me; I was nervous and had trouble settling in, but still I was at the round wooden table at the back of the stacks, hardcover fiction all around me, a high cathedral window in front of me opening into a redwood forest, moving my pen across the page. I am used to beginnings: my mind was jittery, shook up, and I knew it would take a while to settle.

For the entire first week I went to the library at ten AM when it opened and again after an afternoon break until nine PM, when I looked up through the window to see the moon through the red-woods. Long moments of that first week a strong, clear and convincing voice whispered in my ear as I wrote: "I don't want to do this." She said it over and over. I'd heard this same voice for a year and a half and I knew she was not easy to divert. I think that was why I'd unconsciously maneuvered this retreat: to face her. Over my last twenty-five years I have encountered many strong inner opponents to my act of writing. They appeared in many forms: sometimes as seduction, beckoning me to hike in the mountains—after all, it's a beautiful day. Sometimes they're full of recrimina-tions—I am selfish, stupid, unrealistic, my writing will lead to nothing and is a waste of time.

But this was a new voice, and I was beginning to believe her. She consistently hammered home her message: I don't want to do this. She was persistent beyond anything I had faced before. Maybe I needed to honor her. Maybe she was telling the truth—I'd limited my life. Enough was enough. I needed to see what was out in the world beyond writing.

On Sunday when the library closed, I, too, took the day off and went into San Francisco to meet my friend Hillary. She was the only one I got together with in the full three weeks. I knew if I started socializing with dear, old friends I'd be lost.

At the new modern art museum as we looked at a Diebenkorn, then a Joan Brown, an Agnes Martin, a Marsden Hartley, I explained to Hillary, "I have to listen to that voice. When this book is done, I will consider what else there is to do. The voice doesn't feel like resistance, only something honest and real."

Hillary listened closely—a voice that could stop Nat from writ-ing? She'd never heard me like that before.

On Monday morning I stopped as usual at True Confections, a bakery around the corner from the library. During the first week I had quickly developed the habit of going at nine, ordering a hot chocolate and croissant, and re-reading my last two or three pages from the evening before to prepare myself for the day's work. If I was delighted with what I read I ordered a second pain au chocolat. There was good music on the tape recorder in the back of the bakery, and to get to the bathroom, I had the pleasure of crossing through the kitchen where they were frosting a wedding cake, removing brownies from the oven, and lifting with a spatula warm, dark-spotted—either raisin or chocolate chip—cookies from a pan. The bakers began to recognize and greet me—they enjoyed my enthusiasm for their work.

That morning I arrived at the library at ten just as they unlocked the doors. As soon as I sat down at the round table, I exploded with writing—in the old way, in that long love affair with my craft. When I looked up at two o'clock I realized that the strong voice I'd told Hillary about, the voice I was beginning to believe, was gone, dissolved, vanished!

You mean something that forceful for that long, it too was an illusion? I felt humbled—I could have succumbed and lost my true love. I had just been through a big test, but I did not linger over these thoughts. I had writing ahead of me. Was it good? Was it bad? That did not matter—I would consider its use later. For now the old call was here and I was running to it. Monday finished in quiet awe, but writing is work after all, and I was tired afterward.

Back at the flat I opened the windows wide and let the humid night pour into the living room. I lay on the long white couch and read Willa Cather's *The Song of the Lark* for the second time. The story penetrated even deeper than the first time and when Ray Kennedy, the railroad man, died I fell over the pages and cried more than I ever had at a scene in a book. I said to myself, Nat, please, no one you know actually died. But this was no consolation.

Literature poured through me with the exquisite poignancy of life—my body was a conduit rushing words to my heart.

I did not sleep that night. It was as though a great ocean was below my bed—some huge force that alerted my whole being and kept me awake. Tuesday I wrote. Again the writing came in a flood. No resistance—as though my mind had awakened across a great chasm to the call of practice and responded to dailiness and consistency like a child content in an orderly world. But by evening I felt a quiet dread and I did not want to go to bed that night. I knew there would be little sleep.

I awoke in the morning haggard, as though throughout the late hours I had been pulling in with my own small arms heavy steamer ships loaded with coal, but by noon in my library seat the night was far behind me. I had settled deep into the notebook. But Wednesday's sleep was the worst. I battled the pillows, the covers, I tried dragging a quilt into the living room and sleeping on the couch. Then I jumped up. I tried the bed again. I said to myself, this feels like I've just broken up with a long-term lover and am not used to sleeping alone. I felt bereft.

Thursday morning I was miserable, even refusing to drag myself to the library until eleven. I sat in my usual place, having carried over from reference the hefty, red, large-lettered Webster's. I also hauled over the bulky *Synonym Finder* I'd bought—the library hadn't had one. Each evening I hid it among the novels so I wouldn't have to lug it home. Again, the writing flew out of me—I was on an invincible roll by now. But I was personally bedraggled, with a slight headache, puffy eyes and a fearful recognition that a sore throat was on its way. Between my writing self and my human self a Grand Canyon had formed. I wrote abundantly and suffered terribly. I had no name for my sorrow, no understanding of it. I wasn't even sure the two worlds were connected. I was writing about language—why should that arouse such torment? For the last two days I hadn't even re-read what I had written. Instead I blindly began the work each day afraid, with my exhaustion, that if I gave a moment's reflection I'd quit the whole thing.

I left the library at two and walked down a street lined with eucalyptus trees. I thought, Nat, try to pull yourself together—do some slow walking. I turned at an alley thick with low growing ferns and noticed a long steep flight of stairs. I climbed them and when I got to the top I was breathing heavily. I looked up. I could actually see the wind that moved the tops of trees. Pure air had never seemed so alive. Stunned, I bent my head, stumbled to the curb, sat down and began to sob, intermittently glancing up at a line of poplars that tossed and tilted with the wind's vigor. I poured out tears, mucus streamed from my nose. I had no tissues and no idea what was going on. A line from Jack Kerouac ran through my head: "Accept loss forever." It was the only sense I could make of what was happening. My grief was that I held onto everything: good experiences, I didn't want them to go; bad experiences, I clutched them in fear, armoring myself, not wanting them repeated; and then everything in between, small instances, moments, all passing, all fervently known and unknown, held, wanted, struggled with. Everything I loved, everything I didn't love. The contrast between how the writing was moving through me and how I let nothing else budge must have been breaking me. So many people I had loved. All gone. So many good times. Vanished—and held inside.

After a long time I finally stopped crying and stood on shaky legs. I walked home knowing I'd sleep that night—whatever was rumbling beneath the surface had completed itself. Hemingway had said, "Not the why but the what." This is *what* happened on my writing retreat. Why? I can't explain it, only writing opens us wide so that our individual suffering becomes universal suffering. When

I was crying in realization of how I cling to everything, it was a big cry—I knew it was what all human beings do. I was not separate. I felt all our human anguish.

That weekend I walked like a ghost among people. I gave my name as Jane in the Book Depot when they called it out to say my sandwich was ready. A woman came over to me one afternoon, "Aren't you Natalie Goldberg?" "No," I shook my head and looked down. And it was true—I wasn't who I was. I was in a different reality from people moving in their daily life. Mill Valley wasn't my home. I didn't use the phone. I scheduled no meetings. I had one purpose: to write, but through that one act the whole inner world opened to me. I was living out an intimate reality with myself.

Near the end of the last week, I was in a café about to bite into a fat hamburger—my first newspaper since the retreat began propped against a water glass—when I read to my astonishment that Allen Ginsberg had just died. I put down the food and looked out the window. The sun was on trees and sidewalks and parked cars. Our American bard was dead. Tears brimmed my eyes and my throat was tight. He began all this for me a long time ago, I whispered. The breath in my body hurt. I had continued with what he had taught me. I had dedicated myself to making the study of mind through writing a practical step-by-step practice. When I studied with him at Naropa Institute in the summer of 1976, he was the same age I was now. I remembered a haiku he'd written then. I quietly recited it to myself in the plastic booth before the white table with the bustle of the lunch crowd around me and fries crackling in their oil:

> Buddha died and
> left behind a
> big emptiness

All at once I felt cold and got up and left.

We'd taught together twice in Los Angeles in the last five years. He was ever fresh: eagerly taking notes when I lectured, and asking me—this ancient teacher—what I thought of what he planned to teach. We went for breakfast the morning after the workshop. We met in the hotel lobby and he walked slowly, from a stroke he'd had. He was on a strict diet and he studied the menu carefully. He told me about a three-month trip he'd taken through Europe to all his old haunts. When he got to Morocco to visit Paul Bowles, whom he hadn't seen in years, he heard anti-Semitic comments in the streets and felt lonely and wanted to return home.

Later that day I read in another newspaper that when Allen heard he had a short time to live because of the extent of his liver cancer, he cried and then stayed up through the night calling old friends to say farewell. Till the end he continued his writing practice. He wanted to record what it was like to go out peacefully, with acceptance.

Suddenly I trembled from head to toe: I acknowledged how scared I had been to do this retreat. I'd had to trick myself into coming with the idea of being close to good friends in the Bay Area.

That night as I washed my face and got ready for bed, long-buried memories arose whole and luminous, like dead fish coming up to the surface. As I looked into the medicine-chest mirror, I remembered a slam book that had been passed around in sixth grade. It had a mottled black-and-white cardboard cover, so if you were caught it was camouflaged as a composition book. On the first page was a list of numbers. You wrote your name next to one and from then on you were number fourteen. "What do you think of" was written, and then came blank pages, each with someone's name at the top. It could be Marilyn Monroe or . . . Natalie

Goldberg. You could write what you thought about that person any-where on that page—the blue lines didn't matter—and then a slash and your number. On my page were a sprinkling of two or three NICEs, then UGLY/ 18 (John Giocametti), then three HELPs all in squiggly letters like it was Halloween—these from boys. The girls were kinder: OK, SMART.

I remembered looking down at that page, my straight dark hair pulled back in a barrette. My first flash was, I'm not that bad, and then I was stunned into a terrible, deep silence. I closed the book and passed it, never giving myself a number.

I turned out the bathroom light as a rose of pain bloomed in my chest.

As I slipped under the sheets, a face flashed across my mind: it was Ernie Di Giovanni's. I was in eighth grade and Ernie was my best friend Phyllis's older brother. Their father was a garbageman and they were going to work hard in school and make something of themselves. Ernie was seventeen; he had graduated from high school early and was driving alone each day in his white Falcon to Queens College an hour away to take courses. He wasn't prepared for a city school and had no friends there and was lonely. He was handsome: white skin, black hair, dark eyes. He drove me home one early evening after I did schoolwork with Phyllis. He stopped in a lot at Bethpage State Park and turned in his seat, his arm over the back. I couldn't see his eyes in the twilight.

"Natalie, this is awkward. I know you're my sister's friend, but I like you."

I looked down at my hands. "What does that mean?"

"I'd like to date you."

"I can't," I said. He was too close. I was nervous, shocked.

He didn't say another word. He turned away—the clutch in those days was at the steering wheel—and shifted into reverse.

I lay back on my pillow. Ernie had liked me, had noticed me—two lonely people like swans in the night of our teen years. Maybe I wasn't so ugly.

It was unbearable to think of that young Natalie. And yet that evening I reconnected with my one true lineage before all the others: myself. I'd bypassed her, tried to put her to flames when I left home at eighteen, abandoned her when I became a hippie in my early twenties, then rode on my Zen teacher's back to become a writer in my thirties. "I did it for him," I'd say. Now the orphaned one was rising before me. Whom do you write for? I write for you, I answered. To record how you saw and felt before you were silenced.

Whom do you write for? I asked again. I write for myself—and through myself for everyone.

At the library the next day I repeated to myself: Remember her. Stay with her. You have uncovered a true root. Stand with her and you'll be steady on your own feet. You won't wobble. A veil had been lifted. I'd found a home beyond home. I wrote until the half moon appeared at the tops of the two redwoods and then I left, knowing it was my last night.

This retreat wasn't a strict seven-day sesshin (Zen meditation retreat), but the inner content was similar: out alone on a lonesome cliff hanging onto a craggy rock, your hands bleeding. The same wrestling, openings, surrender, the same scraping against yourself, same humbling, final, broken weary acceptance.

This is what I want to make clear here; this is a declaration, a manifesto: writing is a true spiritual path, an authentic Zen way. Writing is an immediate mirror: it reports back to you. You can't fool anyone, especially yourself. Here you are the doer and the done, the worldly person and the monk. It's an opportunity to unite the inner with the outer, both being the same anyway, only in illusion two. A great challenge, a great practice. A large way.

APPENDIX:
BOOKS I LOVE

I am often asked by students and in interviews what books I love. I have read many fine ones over the years, but some walk with me, live with me and have formed my writing life. Here's my list of those:

A Zen Wave by Robert Aitken
The Stupids Die by Harry Allard and James Marshall
The Stupids Have a Ball by Harry Allard and James Marshall
Bastard Out of Carolina by Dorothy Allison
Max Perkins: Editor of Genius by Scott Berg
Crow with No Mouth: Ikkyu by Stephen Berg
Haiku: volumes 1–4 by R. H. Blyth
Weeding the Cosmos by John Brandi
The Lonely Hunter, a biography of Carson McCullers, by
    Virginia Spencer Carr
The Song of the Lark by Willa Cather
Thank You and OK! by David Chadwick
The Paperboy by Pete Dexter

Stones for Ibarra by Harriet Doerr

Miriam's Kitchen by Elizabeth Ehrlich

Children of the Holocaust by Helen Epstein

Love Medicine by Louise Erdrich

The Great Gatsby by F. Scott Fitzgerald

A Lesson Before Dying by Ernest J. Gaines

The Anna Papers by Ellen Gilchrist

Allen Verbatim, lectures by Allen Ginsberg, ed. Gordon Ball

Howl, and other poems by Allen Ginsberg

Kaddish, and other poems, 1958–1960 by Allen Ginsberg

Fierce Attachments by Vivian Gornick

Too Bright to See by Linda Gregg

A Romantic Education by Patricia Hampl

Death in the Afternoon by Ernest Hemingway

A Moveable Feast by Ernest Hemingway

31 Letters and 13 Dreams by Richard Hugo

The Triggering Town by Richard Hugo

French Lessons by Alice Kaplan

At the Bottom of the River by Jamaica Kincaid

A Small Place by Jamaica Kincaid

South of the Big Four by Don Kurtz

Basic Needs by Julie Landsman

What Work Is by Philip Levine

Two Arrows Meeting in Mid-Air by John Daido Loori

Edge of Taos Desert by Mabel Dodge Luhan

The Ballad of the Sad Café by Carson McCullers

Reflections in a Golden Eye by Carson McCullers

The Last Picture Show by Larry McMurtry

Leaving Cheyenne by Larry McMurtry

Under the Tuscan Sun by Frances Mayes

Becoming a Man by Paul Monette

Endless Vow by Soen Nakagawa et al.

An Elegy for September by John Nichols

The Things They Carried by Tim O'Brien

The Shipping News by E. Annie Proulx

After Leaving Mr. Mackenzie by Jean Rhys

Good Morning, Midnight by Jean Rhys

American Pastoral by Philip Roth

Patrimony by Philip Roth

Nine Stories by J. D. Salinger

Light Years by James Salter

The Book of Folly by Anne Sexton

Ceremony by Leslie Marmon Silko

A Thousand Acres by Jane Smiley

Angle of Repose by Wallace Stegner

Crossing to Safety by Wallace Stegner

The Red Coal by Gerald Stern

Roadfood by Jane and Michael Stern

Seeds from a Birch Tree by Clark Strand

Zen Mind, Beginner's Mind by Shunryu Suzuki

The Kommandant's Mistress by Sherri Szeman

The Farm on the River of Emeralds by Moritz Thomsen

Living Poor by Moritz Thomsen

My Own Country by Abraham Verghese

Mississippi by Anthony Walton

The Man Who Killed a Deer by Frank Waters

Montana 1948 by Larry Watson

A Streetcar Named Desire by Tennessee Williams

Departures by Paul Zweig

PERMISSIONS

About the Author

NATALIE GOLDBERG lives in northern New Mexico and is the author of *Writing Down the Bones, Wild Mind, Long Quiet Highway, Banana Rose,* and *Living Color,* a book about her work as a painter. She teaches writing in workshops nationwide.

For information on Natalie's upcoming schedule, visit her website at *www.nataliegoldberg.com.*

WILD MIND

"For fifteen years now, at the beginning of every writing workshop,
I have repeated the rules for writing practice. I will repeat them
again here . . . They are the bottom line, the beginning of all
writing, the foundation of learning to trust your own mind."

In this much-loved guide, Natalie Goldberg lays out the rules for
her unique approach to writing, designed to take you beyond
craft to the true source of creative power: the mind that
is "raw, full of energy, alive and hungry."

0-553-34775-6 $13.95/$21.95C

LONG QUIET HIGHWAY

In this memoir, Natalie Goldberg takes us on a wonderful journey
of awakening from the profound sleep of a suburban childhood.
From the high school classroom where she first listened to the
rain to her fifteen years as a student of Zen Buddhism, she
captures both the moments of illumination and the long
discipline of daily practice as she teaches us that "Every
moment is enormous, and it is all we have."

0-553-37315-3 $13.95/$21.95C

BANANA ROSE

In her remarkable books on the craft of writing, Natalie Goldberg has proved an inspiration to a legion of readers. With insight, humor, and empathy, her writing speaks to the heart. Now in her acclaimed first novel, she explores one woman's coming of age and coming to terms . . .

"After reading *Banana Rose*, you'll be wondering if you haven't just had a pure glimpse of Natalie herself."
—Clarissa Pinkola Estés, Ph.D.,
author of *Women Who Run With the Wolves*

0-553-37513-X $13.95/$21.00C

LIVING COLOR

"What I recall clearly about the first true painting I ever did was the feeling that night that something real was happening. I sensed it in my body, in my hand holding the brush—a dash of yellow in the center, red close to the purple. I moved quickly. The sky outside was dark, the house silent . . . I had let go and let something larger than myself take over."

Join Natalie Goldberg as she takes her unique understanding of the search for the spirit, and transforms it into paintings that come to life with the same exuberance as her writing.

0-553-35489-2 $16.95/$23.95C